Against Human Dignity

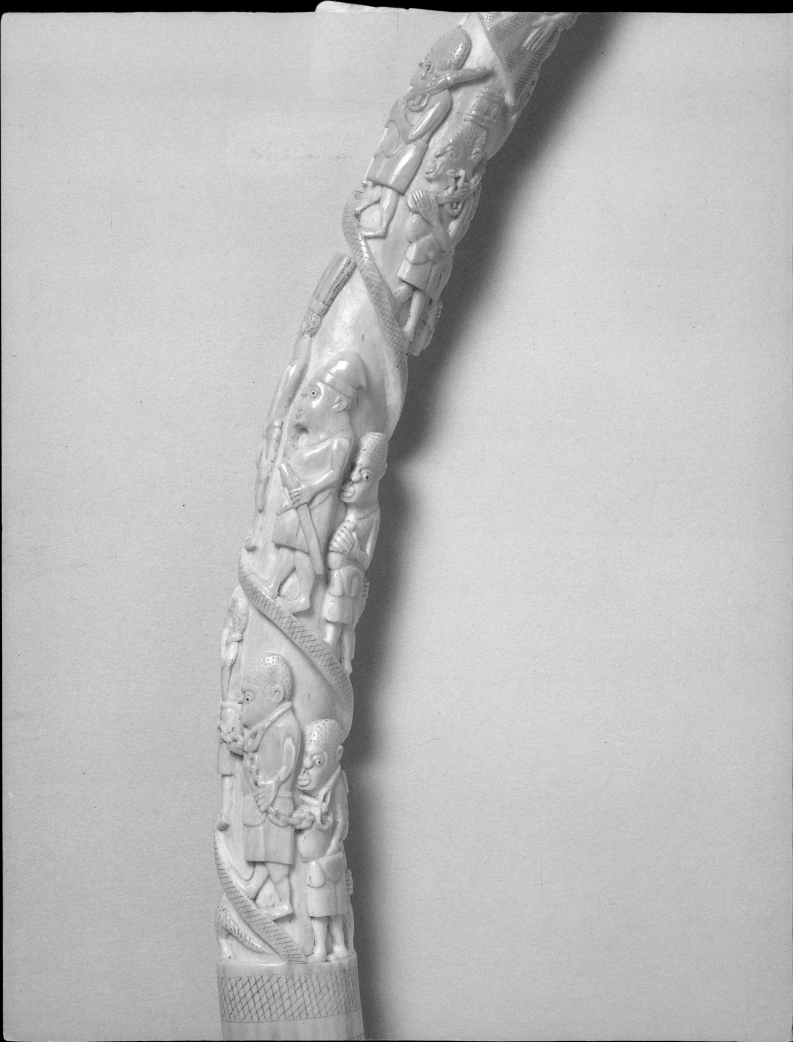

TRANSATLANTIC SLAVERY

AGAINST HUMAN

DIGNITY

Edited by Anthony Tibbles

NATIONAL MUSEUMS & GALLERIES
· ON MERSEYSIDE ·

London: HMSO

This catalogue is published to accompany the opening of the Transatlantic Slavery Gallery at Merseyside Maritime Museum in Liverpool. The Gallery was initiated and has been generously sponsored by the Peter Moores Foundation.

Illustrations of catalogue items appear throughout the text. Full details will be found in the items catalogue, pages 129-165.

ISBN 0 11 290539 0 (paperback)
ISBN 0 11 290545 5 (cased edition)

© National Museums and Galleries on Merseyside 1994
Applications for reproduction should be made to HMSO
Second impression in paperback 1995
All rights reserved
Catalogue prepared by
Merrell Holberton Publishers
in association with NMGM

Design by Roger Davies
Cover design by HMSO:
Melanie Williams

British Library Cataloguing in Publication Data
A CIP catalogue record for this book is available from the British Library

Printed in the United Kingdom for HMSO
Dd 301269 C20 9/95 3396/2 20249

Half title illustration
Cat. 124
Seal, Royal coat of arms of George III, 'OFFICE FOR
REGISTRATION OF SLAVES DEMERARY'
Wax, Demerara

Title page illustration
Cat. 45
Carved ivory tusk, showing chained figures
Gabon, 19th century

Contents

Advisory Committee

Lord Pitt of Hampstead, Chairman

Dame Jocelyn Barrow   Wally Brown (to July 1993)   Angus Chukuemeka
Alissandra Cummins   Richard Foster   Len Garrison
Professor Stuart Hall   Herbie Higgins   Professor Alistair Hennessy
Barbara Johnstone   Professor Preston King   Dorothy Kuya
Sir Shridath Ramphal   Dr Stephen Small   Sir Kenneth Stuart   Alan Swerdlow
Sir David Wilson

Guest Curators' Group

Femi Biko, Lecturer, Lambeth Education Institute, London
Alissandra Cummins, Director, Barbados Museum and Historical Society
Dr Mary E. Modupe Kolawole, Senior Lecturer, African Women's Cultural and Literary Studies,
Obafemi Awolowo University, Ile-Ife, Nigeria
Preston King, Professor of Political Philosophy, Lancaster University
Paul Lovejoy, Professor, Department of History, York University, Ontario, Canada
Patrick Manning, Professor, Department of African-American Studies,
Northwestern University, Boston, USA
Jennifer Morgan, Research Fellow, University of South Carolina, USA
Edward Reynolds, Professor of History, University of California, San Diego, USA
David Richardson, Reader in Economic History, University of Hull
Dr Stephen Small, Lecturer in Sociology, University of Leicester
James Walvin, Professor of History, University of York

NMGM project/curatorial team

Anthony Tibbles, Curator of Maritime History and Project Leader
Alison Taubman, Project Curator
Gail Cameron, Assistant Curator (to August 1993)
Joanne Howdle, Assistant Curator (from November 1993)
Garry Morris, Project Outreach Worker
Paul Rees, Senior Education Officer
Keith Robinson, Senior Designer
Edmund Southworth, Curator of Archaeology & Ethnology
Sally-Ann Yates, Project Co-ordinator for Conservation Division

Consultant Designer
Ivor Heal Design Ltd

Opposite
'Cutting sugar cane' from W. Clark,
Ten Views in Antigua, 1823
(detail of fig. 12)

Lenders to the Gallery

American Museum of Natural History, New York

American Numismatic Society, New York

Anti-Slavery International

Chicago Historical Society

Manchester Museum

Museum of History, Anthropology and Art of the University of Puerto Rico
(Museo Universidad de Puerto Rico)

Museum of Science and Industry in Manchester

National Maritime Museum, London

Norwich Castle Museum, Norfolk Museum Service

Royal Albert Memorial Museum, Exeter

Science Museum, London

Tate & Lyle Sugars plc

Texas Memorial Museum, University of Texas at Austin
(Department of History & Anthropology)

Trustees of the British Museum

Whitehaven Museum

Wilberforce House, Hull City Museums & Art Gallery

Williamson Art Gallery & Museum, Birkenhead

Foreword

During forty years of work and travel in Europe and America, it became increasingly clear to me that slavery was a taboo subject, both to white and to black people. Forty years ago, most Europeans had managed to suppress any acknowledgement of their connection with the slave trade. It was something in the past. In the United States, where it was impossible to ignore the results of the slave trade, there was segregation, later bussing and recently something like integration, but never any mention of how black people came to be in America in the first place. We can come to terms with our past only by accepting it, and in order to be able to accept it we need knowledge of what actually happened. We need to make sense of our history.

It seemed to me that the taboo should be exorcised, and black friends agreed with me. I am pleased that my idea to have a permanent slave trade gallery has been taken up by National Museums and Galleries on Merseyside. It is particularly appropriate that this gallery should be in Liverpool, which not only has one of the oldest black communities in Europe but was also the major European slaving port in the eighteenth century.

A visit to the exhibition is bound to disturb us – black or white. But it is meant to bring the slave trade before us without mincing matters, to act as a catalyst which will spark off reflection, debate, understanding and further study.

During the two years leading up to the opening of the gallery, a distinguished group of people from Liverpool and around the world have worked together to research, debate, advise and guide the project in the right direction. I am grateful for the support which they have given and feel privileged to be associated with these enthusiastic, dedicated and committed people whose work has made this exhibition possible.

PETER MOORES
Patron
Peter Moores Foundation

Foreword

This catalogue is the result of two years of intense discussion and debate on the relationship of slavery to the growth and influence of European power on the continents and islands bordering the Atlantic ocean. The writers look at transatlantic slavery from varying perspectives but common to all positions is the strong sense not only of the horror and brutality of the trade and the denial of personal freedom but of the impact of the wholesale removal of peoples from their homelands, cultures and families. The story of transatlantic slavery is a reminder of one of the more dramatic and far-reaching ways in which the relentless driving forces of commerce and economic nationalism are capable of altering the world order. For Liverpool, whose merchants were by the end of the eighteenth century pre-eminent in this trade, the gains were substantial. Personal and civic prosperity were derived from it, the place names and architecture of the city also reflect its influence.

The long-standing interest of the Peter Moores Foundation in telling this story coincided with the Trustees' desire to respond to a widely held view that the Maritime Museum should re-address the subject of transatlantic slavery. When, therefore, the Foundation approached National Museums and Galleries on Merseyside with the proposal to develop a gallery about the transatlantic slave trade, it was an offer the Trustees readily accepted.

The Transatlantic Slavery Gallery is one of the most challenging projects that NMGM has undertaken. It was bound to be so. The subject touches deeply seated emotions and this is particularly true for black people whose ancestors were subjected to the horrors of slavery. We have been fortunate in enlisting support from many quarters. We have had the steady guidance and advice of a distinguished Advisory Committee meeting under the chairmanship of Lord Pitt of Hampstead. We are also grateful for the assistance of colleagues in many museums in this country and abroad who have agreed to lend objects to the gallery.

In conclusion I would like to thank my colleagues in NMGM, especially Anthony Tibbles who edited the catalogue and who, together with Alison Taubman, prepared the display. They in turn have benefited from the active participation of an international group of guest curators, who have also contributed to this catalogue. Finally, I would like to acknowledge the generous support and encouragement of Peter Moores, whose Foundation provided the resources to establish this new gallery.

RICHARD FOSTER
Director
National Museums and Galleries on Merseyside

Opposite
The Family of Sir William Young (detail of fig. 18 on p. 86)
by Johann Zoffany, NMGM (Walker Art Gallery)

Introduction

In the period between about 1500 and about 1870, millions of Africans were enslaved and transported across the Atlantic by Europeans, who needed a labour force to develop and work in their American colonies. Although this is usually described as the 'Atlantic Slave Trade', we have chosen to adopt the wider, more embracing term 'Transatlantic Slavery' as the title for the gallery, not least because 'slave trade' concentrates on the dehumanising aspects. We have to be able to see beyond the mechanics of the operation and remember that this is a story about people.

The system of transatlantic slavery is often referred to as the Triangular Trade. Seen from this perspective, there were three stages, involving the three continents of Europe, Africa and America. Ships set out from ports on the western seaboard of Europe – from Spain, Portugal, the Netherlands, England, France and even Denmark and Sweden – laden with a variety of trade goods. Arriving on the west coast of Africa, captains exchanged these goods for enslaved Africans. The process often took weeks or months. The second leg of the journey was the infamous 'Middle Passage' from Africa across the Atlantic. On arrival the captives who had survived the voyage were sold and put to work. The final stage of the trade saw the ships returning to Europe with goods, in particular sugar, coffee, tobacco and rice, or with credit notes. The merchants and their investors then took their profits, which supported their life-style or were re-invested in property, land and other new ventures.

But it is not accurate to see the system as always taking a triangular form. There were, for instance, a significant number of bi-lateral voyages between Brazil and Africa, particularly after the official abolition of the trade in the nineteenth century. Nor should it be forgotten that the direct trade between Europe and its American colonies in the seventeenth and eighteenth centuries was equally dependent on slavery. The goods brought back were produced by slave labour, which was sustained by the trade in Africans.

Of course, for the African, the experience was very different. For many of those enslaved the process began away from the coast as they were seized in wars or raids and were sold from one trader to another. They often faced long arduous journeys and few knew what final destination or fate awaited them. On arrival at the coast they were usually imprisoned in forts before being loaded on to ships. Few would have ever seen the sea, or a ship, or a white man before. They found themselves thrown together with people from different parts of Africa, speaking different languages, in conditions of horror, deprivation and violence. In this way they crossed the Atlantic. On arrival in the Americas, they were parted from their shipmates and often their families as they were sold to different owners. Many faced further journeys as they were led to the plantations and other places where they were put to work. The vast majority knew only a life of hard labour ending in death far from home.

The essays which follow are not intended to provide a blow-by-blow account of transatlantic slavery. Most are adaptations of briefing papers prepared for the gallery. They do, however, address many of the key issues involved. Some look at specific topics, some are broader. Some are a synthesis of current research, others adopt a more personal approach. It is my hope that they will cause people to think about transatlantic slavery, to understand the context and to recognise that it has relevance for all of us today.

ANTHONY TIBBLES

Transatlantic Slavery

55
Trade token, inscribed 'Tom Buck of
Grandy Bonny an Honest Trader ...'
Ivory

Illustrations of catalogue items appear throughout these essays
besides supplementary figures. Full details of the catalogue items illustrated will be found, in
numerical order, between pages 129 and 165.

The Rise of the Atlantic Empires

DAVID RICHARDSON

30
Map of Europe and North Africa
Parchment, 16th century

The fifteenth and sixteenth centuries are often described as the 'Age of Discoveries'. Helped by improvements in maritime technology, Portuguese navigators explored the west coast of Africa in the fifteenth century, colonising before 1480 the Atlantic islands of Azores, Madeira and Cape Verde as well as Sao Tome in West Africa. A trading station was then established at El Mina on the Gold Coast of Africa in 1481, before further voyages took the Portuguese into the Indian Ocean after 1498 and across the Atlantic to Brazil in the early sixteenth century. By this date, however, the Genoese-born Columbus had already made three voyages on behalf of the Spanish crown to the West Indies, and from there Spanish interest soon spread to the mainland. Victories by Cortes over the Aztecs in 1521 and by Pizarro over the Incas a decade later helped to create a Spanish empire in the Americas that, by 1550, stretched from Mexico in the north to Bolivia in the south and included Hispaniola and Cuba in the Caribbean.

The voyages that led to the Portuguese and Spanish empires were mainly intended to develop sea-routes to the East, thus removing Europe's dependence on Middle-Eastern Muslim traders for supplies of spices and other Eastern luxuries. However, their Atlantic empires became major sources of wealth for Portugal and Spain in their own right. In both cases, initial efforts to develop production in their Atlantic colonies centred on sugar. Under Venetian and Genoese influence this crop had become widely cultivated throughout the Mediterranean after its discovery by Europeans in the Middle East at the time of the Crusades. However, sugar cane requires all-year-round heat and moisture and growing conditions in the Mediterranean were less than ideal. Better conditions were to be found in Madeira, the Canaries, Sao Tome, the West Indies and Brazil, and encouraged the Portuguese and Spanish, with Italian financial support, to attempt sugar cultivation there. Production began at Madeira in the 1450s and, by 1500, was also under way at Sao Tome and Hispaniola. Spanish interest in sugar cultivation in the Americas diminished, however, in the early six-

6
Scorpion
Gold, Central South America

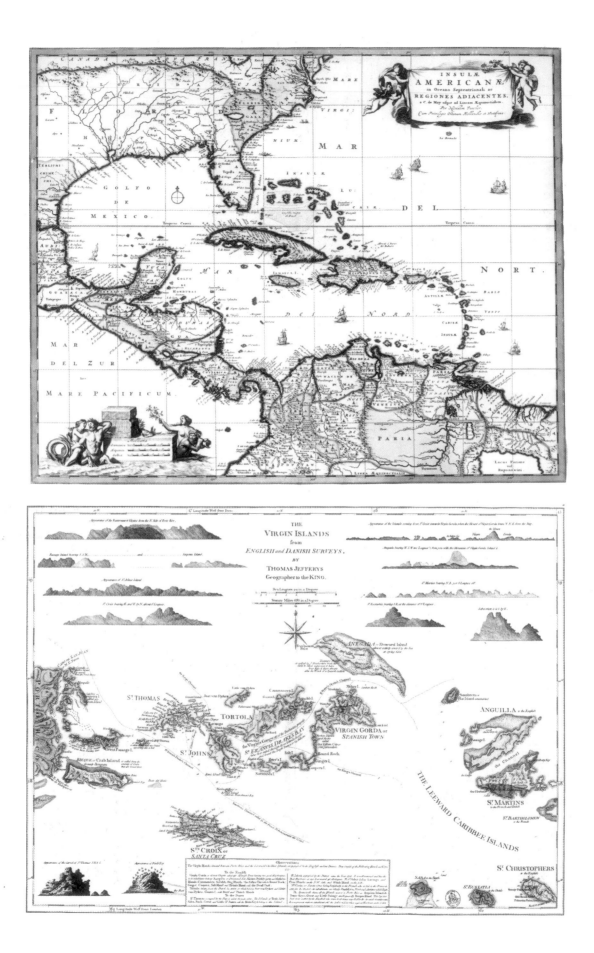

18

100
Chart of Caribbean and Gulf of Mexico, printed and coloured
Nicolas Visscher, Amsterdam, c.1700

7
Idol, two male figures joined at body
Tumbaga, Mexico

106
Map of the Virgin Islands, printed coloured chart
Thomas Jefferys, London 1775

9
Funerary mask with repoussé facial features
Tumbaga, with vestiges of red paint, Sican culture, Peru, c.900 – 1500

67
String of beads
Coral, Benin

63, 64, 65, 70
String of yellow beads with green, red and
blue 'tartan' decoration
Glass

String of yellow beads with green, red and
blue decoration
Glass, Venetian, from Krobo, Ghana

Yellow bead, with green and red
decoration
Glass, from Krobo, Ghana

Trade beads

teenth century as gold and silver began
to flow after the 1520s from mines in
Peru and Bolivia. And until the establishment of sugar and coffee cultivation
in Cuba and Puerto Rico in the late
eighteenth century, silver dominated
exports from Spanish America. However, sugar production in the Portuguese empire spread from the Atlantic
islands to Brazil during the 1540s and
grew rapidly during the following century. Averaging 20-30,000 tons a year,
Brazilian sugar exports dominated the
European market by the 1630s, squeez-
ing out Madeiran and Mediterranean
suppliers and totally overshadowing
sugar production in the West Indies. In
the sixteenth and seventeenth centuries
sugar dominated the Portuguese Atlantic empire as much as silver dominated
the Spanish.

Under the Treaty of Tordesillas,
signed in June 1494, Portugal and Spain
had sought to divide up the world outside Europe, Spain claiming all land
west of a line 370 leagues beyond the
Cape Verde islands, and Portugal all
land east of this line. Ceding Africa and
the then unknown Brazil to Portugal,
the treaty handed the rest of the Americas to Spain. The limited administrative and financial resources of the two
Catholic powers combined with rivalry
between Spain and France in Europe
and the rise of Protestant powers such
as England and Holland to ensure that
Portugal and Spain had little chance of
enforcing their monopoly of the extra-
European world. Portugal's proposed
monopoly on trade to Africa, for instance, was broken in the 1530s by the
French and later by the English adventurers Thomas Wyndham and John
Hawkins. Wyndham made three voyages to Morocco and West Africa in
1551-53 while Hawkins made three
voyages to Sierra Leone in 1562-69, carrying off some 1,200 Africans into slavery. Later, in 1580, Portugal lost its
independence to Spain and before re-
establishing it in 1640 saw the Dutch
gain control in the 1630s of Portuguese
territories in Angola and Brazil.

Despite their superior resources, the
Spanish fared no better than the Portuguese in maintaining their monopoly of
dealings with the rest of the Americas.
Among those infringing Spanish claims

1
Part of beaker with face
Silver, Peru

5, 8
Nose ornament
Gold, South America

Nose ornament
Gold, Columbia

was John Hawkins, who sold the slaves he had taken from Sierra Leone in the 1560s at Hispaniola. And he was followed in the final years of the century by his kinsman, Francis Drake, who made four raids on the Spanish Caribbean between 1570 and 1596. Turning Hawkins and Drake into Elizabethan heroes, these ventures depended on support from the state as well as London's merchant community. Converting private capital into an instrument of the state, they demonstrated how, in the following century, England, Holland and France would create their own formal transatlantic empires. England founded its first colony at Virginia in 1607. Then in the 1620s it added Barbados and the Leeward Islands in the West Indies and began to extend its mainland empire northward to New England and southward into Maryland before seizing Jamaica from Spain in 1655. At the same time, trading factories were established in West Africa at Cormantin (1631) and Cape Coast (1649) on the Gold Coast and James Fort on the Gambia (1661).

While English merchants, courtiers and adventurers were establishing Britain's first colonial empire, their counterparts in France and Holland were creating theirs. Achieving independence from Spain in 1609, the Dutch temporarily seized north-eastern Brazil and Angola in 1629–30 before gaining more permanent possession of Curacao (1634), St Eustatius (1635) and Surinam (1667) in the West Indies as well as trading stations such as El Mina (1637) in Africa. Similarly the French settled Guadaloupe and Martinique in 1635,

107
Map of Curacao printed chart with plan, elevation and six views
Gerard van Keulen, Amsterdam, 1st quarter 18th century

110
Map of St Lucia, printed chart with insets of Carenage, Cul de Sac des Roseaux and Grand Islet
Jacques Nicolas Bellin, Paris 1763

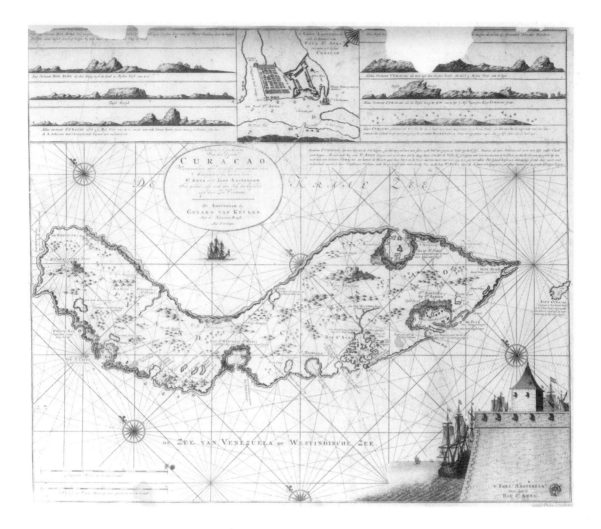

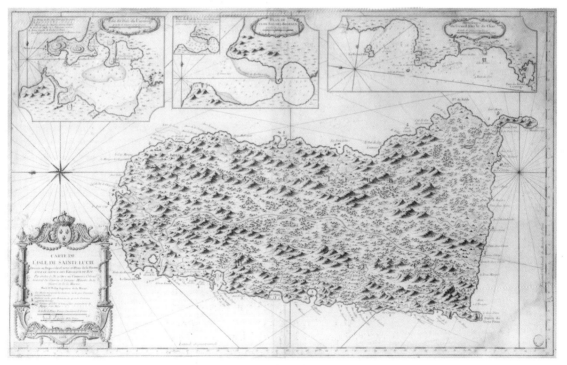

23

Fig.1
Spanish troops conquering the Aztec empire in Mexico, from The Florentine Codex, Spanish, early 16th century

established trading stations in the vicinity of Senegal in the 1670s, and in 1697 formally annexed the greatest prize of all, St Domingue, the western part of Hispaniola.

Thus during the course of the seventeenth century, England, Holland and France had joined Portugal and Spain as major imperial powers in the Atlantic world. Their colonies provided bases from which to acquire through trade or other means the silver and other riches of Spanish America. Colonisation involved, however, significant investment by courtiers and merchants, and from the outset, the founders of most colonies sought to develop cash crops or other goods for export to Europe in order to secure a return on their investments. By 1620, Virginia had begun to produce tobacco for export, and over the following 150 years this became the staple export of the colony as well as of its neighbour, Maryland. Cultivation of tobacco and some other crops was also tried for a time in some of the West Indian islands, but during the mid-1640s sugar cane was introduced to Barbados by Dutch merchants and planters following the expulsion from Brazil by the Portuguese. By 1680 the crop had transformed the island into 'the richest colony in English America'. From Barbados sugar cultivation spread rapidly to the English Leeward Islands and French Martinique and Guadaloupe and then to Jamaica and St Domingue in the early eighteenth century and the Spanish West Indies, especially Cuba, a little later.

Sugar was not, however, the only export from the 'sugar' colonies. Brazil itself experienced a gold boom in 1680-1750 as well as a coffee boom in the nineteenth century, while dye stuffs such as logwood and pimento, ginger, cotton, cocoa and coffee emerged as significant exports from the West Indies between 1660 and 1850. The foundation and development of other colonies outside Brazil and the Caribbean added to the diversification of colonial goods entering transatlantic trade after 1660. Fish, furs and forest products became significant exports from Newfoundland, Quebec and other colonies north of Virginia, while rice and indigo emerged as major exports from the

Fig.2
Spaniards attacking the Aztec city of Tenochtitlan, 1519, from The Florentine Codex, Spanish, early 16th century

Carolinas in the eighteenth century. In addition, from 1790 cotton became a key export from the southern states of the newly established U.S.A., rapidly displacing cotton exports from the West Indies. Despite these developments, precious metals from South America and sugar from Brazil and the West Indies remained the cornerstones of trade from America to Europe until well into the nineteenth century.

The exact scale of such trades can never be determined, but it is estimated[1] that between 1500 and 1800 as much as 100,000 metric tons of silver and 2,500 tons of gold were produced in South America, with over half being produced during the Mexican silver and Brazilian gold booms of the eighteenth century. Figures for sugar[2] suggest that annual exports from the Americas to Europe rose from about 30,000 metric tons in 1650 to almost 200,000 tons in the mid-eighteenth century and to 900,000 tons a century later. Brazil dominated the trade before 1650, Jamaica and St Domingue in the eighteenth century, and Cuba, Puerto Rico, Guyana and a revitalised Brazil in the nineteenth century.

Expanding production and export of precious metals and sugar depended on several factors. These included improvements in ocean-going shipping and navigational skills in Europe, the transfer across the Atlantic of European capital, commercial practices and mining and agricultural technologies, and the seizure by European colonists of property rights over land in America from the indigenous population. The last was achieved largely through military conquest and the elimination, partly through violence but mainly through disease, of many of the indigenous peoples of the Americas. Throughout America, contact with Europeans and exposure to the diseases which they carried led to catastrophic declines in local populations, with some peoples, including the Arawaks and Caribs of the West Indies, disappearing completely.

While such demographic catastrophes facilitated the transfer of rights to land to Europeans, they also deprived the colonists of a potential source of labour with which to exploit the land and

2
Beaker, repoussé decoration of bands with scrolls and birds
Silver, Peru

to earn a profit from it. In most colonies, attempts were made initially to enslave the Indian population, but local resistance to such practices as well as population decline invariably led to their abandonment in favour of recruiting labour from other sources. In the colonies north of Virginia, white labour became the basis of long-term development. Furthermore, the growth of tobacco output in Virginia and Maryland in the seventeenth century also depended heavily on white labour, mainly in the form of indentured servants or convict labour. The former normally worked for four to five years for those who paid for their passage from Europe, while convicts often faced fourteen years of forced labour in the colonies. From their earliest days of colonial expansion, however, the Portuguese and Spanish had turned primarily to enslaved Africans to work their American lands. And when the western European powers began to create and develop their empires in America, they quickly followed the lead given by the Iberian powers.

In retrospect, this seems hardly surprising, for the trans-Saharan slave trade had, by the fifteenth century, long supplied enslaved labour from Africa to work alongside white slaves from Russia and the Balkans on the sugar plantations of the Mediterranean. And with the charting of the west coast of Africa by Portugal in the fifteenth century, an easy supply of controllable labour opened up to the Portuguese to work the sugar plantations they were seeking to establish at Madeira and Sao Tome. Inextricably linking African slaves to European colonial expansion, developments in the Portuguese Atlantic islands in 1450-1500 foreshadowed the pattern of socio-economic development in Spanish America, Brazil, the West Indies and the southern colonies of North America. Over the following four centuries, forced African labour was combined with European capital to exploit the lands and natural resources of the Americas. Thus, the eighteenth-century writer, Malachy Postlethwayt, rightly claimed that the African slave trade was 'the Great Pillar and Support' of British trade with America and that the British empire was 'a magnificent

Fig.3
Caribs attacking the crew of a British ship on St Lucia, 1608, from *Historia Americae* by Theodore Bry, published Frankfurt, 1634. The Caribs were one of the indigenous peoples of the Caribbean. They were enslaved, murdered or died from diseases which Europeans brought with them.

superstructure of American commerce and [British] naval power on an African foundation'.[3] Although related to Britain's empire, Postlethwayt's remarks were equally applicable to the American empires of Portugal, Spain, France and Holland between 1500 and 1850.

1 Ward Barrett, 'World Bullion Flows, 1450-1800' in J.D. Tracy (ed.), *The Rise of Merchant Empires: Long-Distance Trade in the Early Modern World 1350-1750*, Cambridge 1990.

2 Noel Deerr, *The History of Sugar*, 2 vols, London 1949- 50.

3 Malachy Postlethwayt, *The African Trade, the Great Pillar and Support of the British Plantation Trade in America*, London 1745.

4
Figurine
Tumbaga, Columbia

10
Duho
Carved wood, Taino, Caribbean

Human Cargoes: Enslavement and the Middle Passage

EDWARD REYNOLDS

When the Portuguese started to sail down the African coast in the early decades of the fifteenth century, they were aware of the commercial possibilities that the continent offered. They saw opportunities to exploit rich fishing banks and extract quantities of gold from the African peoples. At the same time, the prospect of capturing and selling Africans was not lost upon them. It was the Portuguese who began to capture Africans for export.

In 1441 Antam Goncalves, a Portuguese sailor, seized ten Africans near Cape Bojador. Cited frequently as the beginning of the Atlantic slave trade, this event in 1441 was not formal trade but kidnapping. This type of kidnap-

56
Trade token
Ivory

Fig.4
Slave and traders, Sierra Leone, 1682, from
O. F. von der Groben, *Guineische Reise*, 1694.
A Portuguese merchant (right) is shown
trading for slaves and ivory.

58
Head-dress of cowrie shells with roan
antelope horns
Kon Kombo, West Africa

ping could not be sustained for a long period without retribution from Africans and it later yielded to a formal trade between Africans and Europeans.

Most of the slaves sold to Europeans were acquired through wars and raids. Wars and raids are lumped together because what were often called wars were in fact slave raids. Wars to acquire slaves expanded as the external demand increased. Wars which led to the acquisition of slaves were often motivated by economic gain and African chiefs often weighed the odds of winning and obtaining these benefits before embarking upon such wars. European slave traders encouraged wars through the sale of guns and gunpowder. They were active participants in the wars and conflicts that produced slaves. A slave-ship captain wrote: 'I verily believe, that the far greater part of the wars in Africa, would cease, if the Europeans would cease to tempt them with goods for slaves'. In 1703 the Dutch West Indian Company trading on the Gold Coast supplied the state of Akwamu with one hundred soldiers and firearms to wage war against their neighbours with the resultant slaves going to the Dutch. Warfare for slaves encouraged retaliation and set off a cycle of violence.

Slaves were also kidnapped. Kidnapping was nothing more than stealing a person and, like warfare and raiding, it introduced considerable violence into the society. Unwary individuals, especially women and children, when found alone in isolated places were easy prey for kidnappers. According to a trader: '... an Abundance of little blacks of both sexes were stolen away by their neighbours, when found on roads in the wood'. Such acts of violence no doubt affected trading and other peaceful occupational activities.

Indebtedness led to slavery. When individuals incurred debts and were unable to repay the loans, they were sold into slavery. Even individuals who had been given as pawns (pledges) for debts were not always free from seizure. Slaves were received as tribute by strong states. An area of great misunderstanding is enslavement through the 'judicial process'. Individuals were condemned to slavery for alleged crimes, and by the seventeenth century the laws

30

59
String of cowrie shells
West Africa

62
Gin bottle
Dutch, 18th century

60
Necklace
Hollow tubes of coiled wires, brass, Muni River, Eloby, West Africa

of some societies functioned as a handmaiden to the trade. A traveller reported that: 'The Kings are so absolute, that upon any slight pretense of offense committed by their subjects, they order them to be sold for slaves without regard to rank or profession'. Another traveller wrote: 'Some of the negroe rulers, corrupted by the Europeans, violently infringe the law of Guinea'.

Other infractions that led to enslavement included the practice of witchcraft and the violation of taboos in the society. But the way the 'law' was applied provided room for fraud. Many Africans who were enslaved were not criminals and had violated no laws.

Whatever the method of enslavement, the slaves were marched down from the interior to the forts and factories on the coast that were staffed by Europeans. The slaves arrived in dejected and exhausted condition at the coast, where they were sold through African brokers. Before Europeans could start trading and buying the slaves, it was customary for them to pay duties and give gifts to the African rulers on the coast.

After this exchange of gifts, the slaves were carefully examined from head to toe, without regard to sex, to see that they did not have any blemishes or defects. Some of the slaves were rejected if defects were identified. Among the slavers was a clear preference for fifteen- to twenty-five-year-old males, who represented about two thirds of the slaves.

Most Africans understandably showed extreme levels of distress and despair at being torn away from their homeland, and dreaded what came to be known as the Middle Passage. Some feared that they were being taken away to be eaten by their captors; the attempts by some slavers to explain to the victims the purpose for which they had been purchased failed to allay their fears. Thus some slaves resisted being put on board the slave ships and even tried to drown themselves as they were being taken to the ships.

The conditions on slave ships were slovenly and foul. The height of the decks averaged between four and five feet. In addition to the slave holds, some slavers built half-decks along the sides of the ships, extending no farther than the sides of the scuttles, where slaves, lying in two rows, one above the other, were crowded together and were fastened by leg-irons.

Slaves were brought upon deck at mid-morning and those who had died during the night were thrown into the ocean. The slaves were given water with which to wash, and the ship's surgeon then examined them for sores and other ailments. Meals were served twice daily: breakfast at mid-morning and the other meal late in the afternoon.

To control the hungry captives' food consumption, the process of eating was sometimes directed by signals from a monitor, who indicated when the slaves should dip their fingers or wooden spoons into the food and when they should swallow. It was the responsibility of the monitor to report those who refused to eat, and any slaves found to be attempting to starve themselves were severely whipped. According to a ship's surgeon, "Upon the negroes refusing to take sustenance I have seen coals of fire, glowing hot, put on a shovel, and placed so near their lips as to scorch and burn them". The surgeon continued, "And this has been accompanied with threats, of forcing them to swallow the coals, if they any longer persisted in refusing to eat". At other times, the *speculum orum*, a mouth opener, was used to force-feed the slaves.

Log books were kept on the ship's provisions. These records were vital, since the vessel's capacity did not allow for emergency provisions. Thus, when bad weather prolonged the Middle Passage, food and water allowances were reduced. In September of 1781, the slave ship *Zong* sailed from West Africa with a cargo of 470 slaves bound for Jamaica. Twelve weeks later, as it neared its destination, it ran short of water and food. There was also an outbreak of disease on the ship. When the captain saw impending disaster, he proposed jettisoning those slaves who in his view were too sick to recover, reasoning that the insurance underwriters, rather than the owners, would bear the loss. Furthermore, he argued that the action would save slaves from lingering

77
Sample of brocaded silk
c.1770-80

Fig.5
Africans being forced to 'dance' on board ship, from *France Maritime* by Grehan Amedée, Paris, 1855
"While they are upon deck it is thought necessary that they should take exercise; for which purpose the chief mate and boatswain are stationed with a cat of nine tails, to compel them to dance, as it is called." (William James, third mate on *Britannia*, 1768)

73
Four queen manillas
Copper

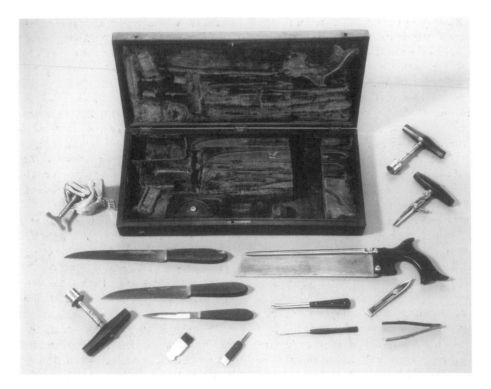

98
Surgical instrument set
London, late 18th/early 19th century

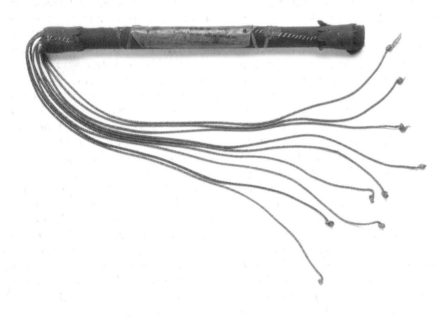

92
Cat-o'-nine-tails
Late 19th century

deaths. One hundred and thirty-six slaves were dragged to the deck and flung overboard. Later the underwriters refused to carry the loss.

The constant threat of disease at sea caused captains to maintain some measure of cleanliness and employ doctors. Slave cargoes were afflicted by fevers, dysentery and smallpox, with smallpox having particularly disastrous effects, since there was no cure for it. To those health dangers may be added the torments of seasickness and the oppressive heat in the holds.

Given the oppressive conditions and the yearning for freedom, slaves inevitably revolted against their ordeal. The fear of slave mutinies led to strict controls and stubborn captives were severely punished. Although all would have welcomed the opportunity to escape, slaves from certain areas earned a reputation for rebellion. The so called 'Coromantees' of the Gold Coast were particularly known for their pride and mutinous behaviour. Often, slaves sought to kill the European traders and set the vessel ashore. Slavers went to great lengths to prevent rebellions and mutinies, visiting the holds daily and searching every corner between the decks for pieces of iron, wood or knives gathered by the slaves. Great care was taken not to leave lying about any object that could be used as a weapon.

Rebellions, contagious diseases, and lack of adequate food compounded the discomfort and difficulty of the passage, which took many African lives. An estimated three to five per cent of the slaves died before embarkation and another eighteen per cent died during the Middle Passage. But this high mortality rate was reduced to about six per cent towards the end of the eighteenth century through efforts to achieve better living conditions on ships. Mortality often depended upon the length of the journey to the Americas and the incubating period of diseases, in addition to the conditions aboard ship.

The mortality rate among the crew of the slavers was high. Although death among the slavers did not exceed that of slaves, there was a correlation, which suggests that they were similarly affected by conditions of disease, faulty provisions and length of voyage.

'Guineamen': Some Technical Aspects of Slave Ships

M. K. STAMMERS

'Guineamen' or slave ships were always typical sailing cargo ships of their time up until the abolition of the trade. After that, extreme designs which made speed of sailing to avoid capture the priority over cargo capacity were introduced. These came in a wide range of sizes. They had to sail reasonably well to shorten the Middle Passage as much as possible, and at the same time they had to have sufficient cargo capacity for trade goods and plantation products. They also needed sufficient stability to carry armaments to defend themselves.

Voyages by European mariners were limited by the size, construction and rig of their vessels until the fifteenth century. From about 1450, existing designs such as the 'cog' and the 'hulc' were overtaken by a new type – the full rigged ship. The 'ship' was at the root of all later developments until the invention of iron-hulled, steam-powered vessels in the nineteenth century. Without it, the slave trade would not have been possible. This new ship design was superior in seaworthiness, sailing ability, size, economy and range of operation to any of its predecessors. Its predecessors were 'shell-built', with their outer skin of planks joined together at their edges. This 'shell' was then made rigid by the insertion of strengthening frames. The new ship was built the other way round. A skeleton consisting of a backbone or keel with stem, sternposts and frames was erected and this was covered with a skin of planks. This change enabled bigger, stronger ships to be built that could carry guns and sufficient men and supplies for long voyages. The implications for long-distance exploration and commercial exploitation are obvious.

It seems likely that this skeleton building technique was first started on the Atlantic coasts of Spain. Allied with it was the introduction of the three-masted sailing rig. In its basic form, this carried square sails on the bowsprit projecting ahead of the ship and on the fore and main masts, and a triangular fore-and-aft lateen sail on the mizzen mast at the stern. The combination of square and fore-and-aft sails made the vessel far more manoeuvrable than its more simply rigged predecessors. Again, like the hull, it was capable of elaboration and development. The first full rigged ships were carracks. Columbus's *Santa Maria*, which opened up the Atlantic for European exploitation, was probably of this build.

The other important feature of the new ship was that because it was simply built of natural materials, it was self-sustaining. There was virtually nothing aboard that carpenters, blacksmiths or sailmakers in the crew could not renew or repair. Given a sheltered beach, the ship's hull could be careened – cleaned of marine growth, re-caulked and repaired. Spare baulks of timber lashed on deck could be fashioned into replacement masts and spars after storm damage, and bolts of spare canvas could be cut and sewn into new sails.

Within a century of its appearance, the European skeleton-built ship had been sailed right round the world and become the essential vehicle for the opening up of the Americas. That of course included the transport of slaves from Africa. The carrack design was gradually superseded in the sixteenth century. The high bow and stern superstructures made the carrack a formidable floating fortress but at the cost of seaworthiness. The galleon design was narrower and longer in the hull. The high bow structure was removed and the reduction in weight helped to lift the bow, so ensuring the passage of the vessel through the seas. Another feature was an extended platform or beakhead below the bowsprit – a feature continued on eighteenth-century ships in a shortened form.

The invention of the 'fluyt' by Dutch shipbuilders about 1600 was the next important development. It was designed as a commercial bulk carrier without the possibility of conversion to an armed vessel. It was flat bottomed, had a higher length to breadth ratio (4:1 up to 6:1), lower superstructure, modest sail plan (to save on crew) and was of lighter construction. It was one of the reasons why the Dutch were able to dominate European sea-trade in the seventeeenth century. Many fluyts passed into English ownership as prizes in the mid-century naval wars, and many of their features were incorporated into their English-built successors.

88
Armed Brig in the Mersey
About 1810, by John Jenkinson (active 1790-1821), oil on canvas, signed

84
GRAND TURK
Exhibition model by W. G. Leavitt, of Salem,
Massachusetts

86
Ship bowl, 'Success To The Dobson 1770'
Tin-glazed earthenware, Liverpool, 1770

However, the fluyt was a slow carrier of low-cost bulk cargoes such as coal, grain or timber, and, although they were used by the Dutch for slaving, they were not particularly successful. In fact, the Dutch used a wide variety of vessels: *hekboot* ('hog boat'), *katschip* ('cat'), *pinas* ('pinnace'), *fregat* ('frigate') and *bark* ('barque') in the late seventeenth century. In 1675, the 'jagt' was reckoned to measure 60 feet (18.3 m) in length, the *fregat* 75 feet (22.9 m) and the bark 110 feet (33.6 m).[1]

The 'jagt' was a single-masted vessel with a fore-and-aft rig. Fore-and-aft sails such as triangular staysails (or jibs) were carried on the fore-and-aft standing rigging that supported the masts. Its gaff mainsail was a large quadrilateral sail which was stretched between two spars, a gaff at the top and a boom at the bottom; both pivoted on the aft side of the mast. The combination of gaff mainsail and staysails at the bow made for a highly manoeuvrable, weatherly vessel pointing up into wind as much as 45° as against 60° for a square rigged vessel. But the majority of slaving vessels were square-rigged.

In the seventeenth century, fore-and-aft sails were added to square-rigged types such as the ship and bark (both three masts) and the 'snow' and 'brig' (both two masts) with resulting improvements in their ability to sail closer to the wind. On long ocean voyages where the wind patterns were relatively constant (for example the Trade Winds in the Atlantic), the square sails came into their own. During the eighteenth century, as the vessels became larger their number increased; so from a main or lower square sail and a topsail in the sixteenth century, masts increased in height for topgallant and royal sails. Light-weather sails known as studding sails which were extended out on spars from the normal sails were introduced in the sixteenth century. These are well illustrated in the sail plan of the *Hall* of 1785. The older method of reducing the size of the main sails by 'bonnets', which were additional pieces of canvas laced to the bottom of the sail, was phased out by 1750 in favour of 'reef points'. These were short lengths of rope sewn into the sails by which the area of the sail could be reduced to stop the vessel labouring in an increasing wind.

Although there were quite a number of small vessels (as small as 20 tons) in the long distance trades, the size of the typical vessels slowly increased in the seventeenth and eighteenth centuries. It is impossible to make a comparison across the main slaving nations because of the differences of tonnage measurement. Even for the English merchant marine alone it is difficult because of the changes in the measuring which in any case was fairly inexact before the Registry Act of 1786.[2] As no more than an indication of the changes, the average size of Liverpool vessels according to Stewart-Brown[3] changed thus:

1709	70 tons burthern
1751	under 90 tons burthern
1765	100 tons burthern
1785	under 140 tons burthern
1795	under 160 tons burthern
1800	under 200 tons burthern

This included small coastal traders; but the situation varied from port to port. London, which dominated English shipping in 1700, had large bulk vessels in the east coast trade as well as the very large ships of 400 to 500 tons working for the East India Company. On the whole, there is an impression that the slave ships tended to be larger than average, and towards the end of the era there is a distinction between a West Indiaman which was trading directly and tended to be London-built and a Guineaman engaged in the slave trade which was largely Liverpool or Bristol built or owned. However, there were exceptions to this, for example in the case of Lancaster slave ships there was a specialisation in smaller brig or snow-rigged vessels.[4] Gomer Williams has a table on the number and tonnage of Liverpool slave ships clearing the port between 1709 and 1807. Unfortunately, he did not give his sources and they must be treated cautiously. They seem to indicate that Liverpool Guineamen after 1730 were always larger than the average ship of the port:[5]

1709	30 tons
1730	74 tons
1751	104 tons
1765	113 tons
1785	139 tons
1797	226 tons
1800	281 tons

Other European slaving ports seem to have owned vessels of similar size to the Liverpool ones. French ships at Nantes, Bordeaux, etc, were between 200 to 400 tonnes, and the Dutch and Danish vessels lay in a similar range.[6]

The hull shape of a vessel put into the slave trade had to combine a fair turn of speed for the Middle Passage and to avoid attack by enemy warships or privateers with a need to carry a large return cargo from the West Indies. Plans and half-models have survived from 1770 which provide a more detailed view. The half-model of the *Alexander* in the Science Museum's collection at London has fine lines with a sharp bow, raised floors amidships and a good run aft. She is pierced for eighteen guns and has large hatches which suggest she may have been a Guineaman. The lines

85
WATT
Contemporary builders' model, 1797

plan of the French *Joly* in the Guibert Collection at the Mariners' Museum, Newport News, are even finer.[7] On the other hand, the plan of *Exeter* built at Bristol in 1776 by the Hilhouse family shows a much bluffer hull.[8] The plan of the *Hall* built in Liverpool in 1785 as a West Indiaman which was occasionally dispatched to West Africa was reproduced in 1794 by William Hutchinson in his *Treatise on Naval Architecture*. Hutchinson was the dockmaster at Liverpool who had been a successful privateer commander in his time. His work was one of a growing number of publications on naval architecture. The illustration of the *Hall* includes a sheer elevation, sail and lines plan and, taken in conjunction with the famous plan of the Liverpool ship *Brooks* of 1781, drawn for Parliament in 1786, gives a fairly complete picture of a Liverpool Guineaman of the last quarter of the eighteenth century when that port dominated the business. Their respective dimensions from Liverpool Customs Register were:[9]

	Brooks	Hall
length	99.8ft (30.4m)	103ft (31.4 m)
breadth	26.7ft (8.1 m)	29.5ft (9 m)
depth of hold	5.6ft (1.7 m)	5ft (1.5 m)
tonnage	320	375

The tween-deck height where the enslaved Africans were consigned was 5'8" in the *Brooks* and 5'7" in the *Hall*. The *Brooks* plan also shows a platform in the tween deck which projected six feet out from the sides of the ship. She was described as 'frigate built' which meant she was built with a raised after deck.[10] The *Hall* was similar and one suspects that this was a necessary feature of any Guineaman because it gave the master and crew a raised position of defence against revolt, which was reinforced with swivel guns and a barricade whilst at anchor off the West African coast. The *Hall* mounted 22 guns which appears to have been a typical armament – nine-pounders were the most popular size but many had two or four larger-calibre pieces. It seems certain that both ships were designed with slaving as one possible trade; the press notice of the launch of the *Parr* at Liverpool on 18th November 1797, of 566 tons the largest Guineaman, remarked: 'She is looked upon by judges to be a very beautiful vessel and the largest out of this port in the African trade for which she is designed'.[11]

On the other hand, an advertisement for the sale of the French prize *La Vénus* in Gore's *General Advertiser* of 8th January 1801 described her as 'French-built, sails astonishingly fast' and suitable for either a 'voyage for rice or a compleat Guineaman'. She measured 107 feet 'aloft' (on the main deck), with hold and two decks, 22 guns and a tonnage of 480 tons. Even in the decade immediately before the British abolition, Guineamen could be either purpose-built or conversions.

The last quarter of the eighteenth century witnessed other improvements, of which the most important was the introduction of copper sheathing. Tropical marine boring molluscs, especially the teredo worm, were a major source of damage, especially because a ship might have to spend months at anchor delivering and collecting its freight. The round voyage could take at least a year. Sacrificial wood sheathing had been used from the late seventeenth century along with a mixture of tallow and sulphur. In about 1779, the Royal Navy introduced an improvement by which all the iron bolts in a ship's hull below the waterline were replaced by copper ones. This made it possible to cover the lower hull with thin copper plates without causing electrolytic action between the iron and copper. The method was so effective that it was rapidly adopted by merchant ships sailing to the tropics. The shortage of suitable ship timber caused the gradual introduction of iron knees (brackets) and hold pillars from about 1790 onwards. Iron anchor cables, which were not only stronger but took much more wear than the traditional hemp cables, were available from about 1800 although rare in merchant ships.

There were also attempts to improve the conditions for the Africans on board. This was partly through limitation of numbers by legislation but also through attempts to improve the ventilation of the slave decks. William Jackson's painting of a Liverpool Guineaman of about 1780-1790 shows a line of ports below the gun deck; and the painting of the Danish ship *Fredensberg* of 1787 in the Kronberg Museum shows three large canvas windsails used to force air down the hatches to the Africans below. Boats were also essential to carry cargo and personnel to and from the shore because apart from the home ports like Liverpool, most trading was carried out on anchor. They had to be capable of being rowed and sailed, and in calm weather they were used to tow the ship. The largest could be over 30 feet (9.1 m) long and were rigged as two-masted schooners. They had broad shallow hulls for easy beaching and for stability when carrying. One built by Daniel Brocklebank in 1806 was designed to carry up to 21 hogsheads of sugar.[12]

1. J. M. Postma, *The Dutch in the Atlantic Slave Trade 1600-1815*, Cambridge 1990, pp. 142-48.

2. D. R. MacGregor, *Fast Sailing Ships, their design and construction, 1775-1875*, 2nd edition, London 1988, pp. 23-25.

3. R. Stewart-Brown, *Liverpool Ships in the 18th century*, Liverpool and London 1932, p. 19.

4. M. Elder, *The Slave Trade and the Economic Development of 18th century Lancaster*, Halifax 1991, pp. 40-41.

5. G. Williams, *History of the Liverpool Privateers and Letters of Marque with an account of the Liverpool slave trade*, London and Liverpool 1897, p. 628.

6. J. Boudriot, in *Les Anneaux de la Mémoire*, Nantes 1992, pp. 18-19; Postma, *op. cit.*, pp. 142-48; P. Petersen, *Danskernes Slaver*, Kronberg 1983, p. 19.

7. MacGregor, *op. cit.*, p. 35.

8. Hilhouse Collection, National Maritime Museum.

9. These are Customs House Register dimensions and tonnages; the description of the *Brooks* quoted by Gomer Williams, *op. cit.*, p. 585, and the dimensions of Hutchinson's plan of the *Hall* are slightly different. Liverpool Customs Registers, Merseyside Maritime Museum.

10. W. Falconer, *An Universal Dictionary of the Marine*, London, 1780, p. 134: 'implies the disposition of the decks of such merchant ships as have a descent of four or five steps from the quarter deck and forecastle into the waist ...'.

11. Quoted in Stewart-Brown, *op. cit.*, p. 129.

12. Brocklebank Collection, Merseyside Maritime Museum.

87
A Liverpool Slave Ship
About 1780, by William Jackson, (active about 1780-1803), oil on canvas, signed

African Resistance to Enslavement

STEPHEN SMALL
AND JAMES WALVIN

Introduction

Though the slave trade was horrible and morally repugnant, it did not break the spirit, initiative or resilience of the Africans that suffered the rape of their societies and human resources. Africans resisted their bondage from the moment of enslavement; in fact the history of slavery can be written in terms of slave resistance. Africans have always refused to submit to enslavement and have utilised diverse tactics for asserting their humanity and affirming their dignity. Resistance to European domination began from the very point at which Europeans in Africa tried to enslave Africans; and it continued at all times that slavery prevailed.

Any appreciation of African resistance to enslavement must consider the wide range of types of resistance employed by Africans, and people of African origin, to the economic, physical and psychological subordination and humiliation that was part and parcel of enslavement. Resistance to enslavement was collective and it was individual; it was spontaneous and it was planned; it was physical and violent, and it was passive; it was ideological and it was psychological. Resistance was carried out by men, by women and by children; and it took place at local, national and international levels. We need to look at slaves as well as at black people legally defined as free. We also need to consider the less sensational types of resistance on a day to day level, as well as some of the more sensational rebellions and insurrections. An understanding of resistance reflects Africans' remarkable resilience against the odds, and helps us to understand the institutions and ideologies developed by black people after slavery was formally abolished.

Africa and the Middle Passage

As enslaved Africans were passed down, in Africa, from their captors to the white traders on the coast, many tried to run away. They tried to escape from the coastal baracoons and slave factories where they were kept before sale to the Europeans. Africans saw their greatest opportunity for escape when being passed across the geography and terrain which was their own. But it was also at this time that the Europeans were at their most vigilant.

The most elaborate precautions against slave runaways and revolt were to be found in the slave castles on the African coast. The castle at Cape Coast in 1682 was 'cut out of the rocky ground, arched and divided into several rooms' underground in such a way that it easily imprisoned a thousand Africans.

Attempts at escape did not cease when Africans had been shackled into the holds of ships. The slave ships were permanently on guard against rebellious slaves, most of whom were ever ready to capitalise on the negligence of their captors. Consequently, revolts on slave ships were commonplace. The greatest danger came at meal and exercise times when Africans exploited their greater freedom of movement.

The slave ship's guns were often trained on its own decks; a reminder that the greatest danger was posed by its own human cargo. The slave captains could never rest easy. On a crossing in 1750, John Newton, a Liverpool slave captain, noted in his journal that he had 'made a timely discovery today that the slaves were forming a plot for insurrection. Surprised two of them attempting to get off their leg irons ...'. On this occasion, a young slave tried to pass a spike through the deck gratings to other slaves. Twenty of them managed to break their chains, but Newton's crew were able to prevent the revolt.[1]

Africans often organized an attack on their kidnappers to seize control of the ship. Sometimes they even succeeded in taking over the entire ship. A well known example of a successful revolt aboard ship was that of the *Amistad*. In 1839 over 50 slaves, led by Joseph Cinque, took control of a Spanish slave ship, the *Amistad*, and tried to sail it to Africa. They were captured by an American ship before being transported to a United States court and freed to return to Africa.

When they could not seize control of the ship, Africans sometimes jumped overboard, preferring to die rather than to continue in chains.

Death of Capt. Ferrer, the Captain of the Amistad, July, 1839.

Don Jose Ruiz and Don Pedro Montez, of the Island of Cuba, having purchased fifty-three slaves at Havana, recently imported from Africa, put them on board the Amistad, Capt. Ferrer, in order to transport them to Principe, another port on the Island of Cuba. After being out from Havana about four days, the African captives on board, in order to obtain their freedom, and return to Africa, armed themselves with cane knives, and rose upon the Captain and crew of the vessel. Capt. Ferrer and the cook of the vessel were killed; two of the crew escaped; Ruiz and Montez were made prisoners.

Fig.6
'Death of Capt. Ferrer, the Captain of the *Amistad'*, July 1839, from J.W. Barber, *A History of the Amistad Captives*, 1840
The *Amistad* was taking slaves between ports in Cuba when it was seized by captives who tried to return to Africa

Slave societies

As soon as they were landed in the colonies, Africans resisted in a wide variety of different ways. The most pervasive and persistent form of resistance was small-scale, individual and not always dramatic, including working slow, sabotage and running away. Slaves 'went slow' (that is, they were 'artful' in the planters' words; 'playing fool to ketch wise' as the Jamaican proverb maintains), feigning sickness and infirmity; they worked at their own pace, or pretended not to understand instructions - all to the fury of their owners. Slaves frequently spat, urinated in and polluted the masters' food; they also, in moments of desperation, struck back, responding to blows with blows, to curses with curses. Women in particular frequently handed out verbal abuse to whites. Slaves sometimes tried to hurt their owners without getting caught, poisoning their food, harming their children, their property, their animals.

A persistent feature of resistance was running away. The vast majority ran away for short periods, to see family members, friends or loved ones; others escaped for long periods, sometimes years, even decades. Some slaves were never recaptured. Slaves close to the sea or rivers were likely to escape by water; others fled by foot, cart or any other vehicle available. Whatever the

practical difficulties, slaves ran away as long as slavery existed, and local newspapers carried regular advertisements for runaway slaves. But running away was not without its consequences: if caught they were severely beaten, disfigured or mutilated. The fate of unsuccessful runaways stood as a terrible reminder of what might happen to them.

There were other tragic and heartrending extremities of resistance – suicide and infanticide – as Africans killed themselves or their loved ones rather than live as slaves. A poignant story is told of Margaret Garner who, having escaped to Ohio from Kentucky in 1856 and been tracked down, killed her daughter (almost decapitating her in an attempt to cut her throat) rather than see her enslaved again. "I will go singing to the gallows rather than be returned to slavery", she insisted.[2]

Another form of resistance was largescale, collective and dramatic. Revolt was the most spectacular form of slave resistance; it was also – obviously – the most dangerous. It rarely succeeded. More often it incurred the violent fury of slave owners and the colonial authorities. The risks slaves were prepared to take, and the punishments they were prepared to endure, is a statement of how far freedom was cherished.

The number of slave revolts is hard to calculate because it depends on the definition. For example, in the United

States, calculations range from nine to two hundred and fifty. Revolts were frequent in the British colonies: in Jamaica, the First Maroon War of 1730-40; in Antigua 1735-36; Stono's Rebellion in South Carolina in 1739; Tackey's Revolt in Jamaica in 1760, which cost about sixty white lives and saw the death of four hundred slave rebels, another one hundred executed and five hundred more transported; Jamaica's Second Maroon War of 1795-96 and Fedor's Rebellion in Grenada in 1795-97.

Curiously, some of the most serious revolts occurred after the slave trade had been abolished in 1807. Bussa's Rebellion in Barbados in 1816 was followed by a revolt in Demerara (Guyana) in 1823 and finally, on the eve of slave emancipation, the Baptist War in Jamaica in 1831-32, the most devastating of all. At its height it involved some 20,000 slaves. The fourteen white deaths provoked a violent reprisal which cost five hundred slave lives. The most successful slave revolution was that of Toussaint L'Ouverture in St Domingue in 1791, which led to the establishment of the independent black republic of Haiti.

For most of the history of British slavery, slave revolts were primarily uprisings of Africans and it was only towards the end of slavery (in 1838) that local-born slaves began to play a more leading role. This is understandable in many ways; it was, after all, the Africans who had experienced a life elsewhere and who had endured (and survived) the Atlantic crossing. In the United States 'most leaders were young, literate, married, charismatic men', says Blassingame.[3]

All slave societies had their slave conspiracies, though many of those conspiracies were often the imagination of the whites, ever fearful of their slaves. Any unexplained illness, accident or misunderstood gesture or word was construed as a conspiracy and threat. Wherever conspiracy was imagined or seen, white reprisals were swift and terrible. Whenever revolt actually flared, the planters suppressed it with massive and bloody reprisals and a gruesome tit-for-tat. Slaves knew that if they revolted, they and many others would pay with their lives, normally after excruciating violence. Tackey's Revolt in Antigua in 1735-36 led to at least 86 slaves' executions – 77 of them burned alive. In Barbados in 1816 some four hundred slaves were executed; in Demerara in 1823 (in a revolt which involved perhaps 12,000 slaves) some 250 slaves were executed.

From first to last slaves revolted; from first to last they were repressed with an even greater violence. But the fear of death, violence and torture was not enough to quell the spirit for freedom and this dismal litany of violence continued as long as slavery survived in the colonies. And in time, that violence contributed to the planters' undoing. By the early nineteenth century, such levels of reprisals were completely out of kilter with contemporary British feelings. Many in Britain felt that if slavery could only be kept in place by such massive (and counter-productive) acts of violence, perhaps the time had come to end slavery itself.

Maroon communities

One of the most impressive successes of running away was the maroon communities. Maroon communities were free settlements of ex-slaves who lived independently and often waged war on neighbouring planters and other white settlers. These communities were found from very early times in some of the large islands and less settled colonies. As time passed, maroon commu-

Fig.7
Joseph Cinquez addressing his compatriots on board the Spanish schooner, *Amistad*, 26 Aug 1839.
The crew of the *Amistad* steered the ship to the North American coast. Although captured and tried, Cinquez and his followers were acquitted because they had been illegally enslaved.

178
25 centimes, obverse: palm tree and trophy of arms and flags, reverse: '25c' in snake 'REPUBLIQUE D'HAYTI AN 13'
Silver, Haiti, Petion Republic, 1816

nities were to be found across the entire spread of the Americas. The whites found it difficult to dislodge and defeat the maroons.

The largest and longest lasting maroon settlements were in areas were whites were small in number and the geography was mountainous, such as South and Central America and the Caribbean. In South America massive communities, some numbering tens of thousands, were to be found from as early as the sixteenth century. But recent evidence from the United States has demonstrated that maroon communities were evident throughout the swamps and mountains of the South, where several communities continued for years raiding plantations, attacking and murdering whites.

Cultural resistance

Resistance was achieved, in the cultural realm, specifically in the areas of religion, music and folk-tales, humour and writing. Africans resisted by sustaining their own collectively created worlds and building for themselves a world far removed from the horrors of their daily lives. These different cultural forms share many aspects in common: as social pastimes and human creativity, as a means to communicate information, ideas, insights, openly or furtively, as commentary and critique on life, and as a vision of the future. In this way, cultural practices supplied the fortitude to confront the harsh realities, and were also a means to retaliate against slave masters in ways not immediately obvious, and thus insulate the slave from retaliation.

The consolidation and transformation of African religions, shaped and sometimes overwhelmed by Christianity, were a source of inspiration. Africans embraced and maintained African religious practices, despite the punishments; both slaves and free blacks established churches, forging spiritual and psychological links with one another. Religion and religious leaders were not just a means of spiritual escape; they were often the mediums through which individuals or groups organized themselves for physical escape. Churches could and did sow the

seeds of discord among slaves, particularly those with all black congregations. Collectively religion provided a framework for black organization and self-expression and served as a training ground for black leaders.

Folk-tales across the Americas were clearly influenced by the West African culture in which folk-tales were one of the most important forms. Animal stories pervaded West Africa, including the Nigerian tortoise, the Ghanaian spider (or Ananse) and the rabbit. Such creatures were invariably looked down upon by stronger animals, but they invariably outwitted them by being wise, patient and cunning. Parallels with daily life were not lost.

Music and humour fulfilled many of the same functions, communicating ideas and criticizing the slave system and the Europeans that upheld it, and acting as a means of escape from the harshness and depression often caused by slavery. They also enabled the enslaved Africans to attack the system under which they were forced to serve. In humour, there are numerous examples in which blacks made the master look stupid or ignorant, but in a way that only his acceptance or acknowledgement of this would enable him to respond.

The many efforts to read and write, and to use a pen as a means of communication, uplift and encouragement, also characterized slave resistance, from the humble efforts of slaves to learn the basics of reading and writing to the establishment of schools, newspapers and journals by free blacks. Such efforts, widespread though illegal and severely punished by whites during slavery, carried on relentlessly.

Free blacks

There were many black people in slave societies who were not legally slaves. The so called 'free blacks' were legally free from slavery, but were often subject to identical laws and restrictions of their rights. Particularly in the United States, free black people in the nineteenth century organized and mobilised to end slavery and to secure full equality. This resistance took many forms; some fought for the abolition of slav-

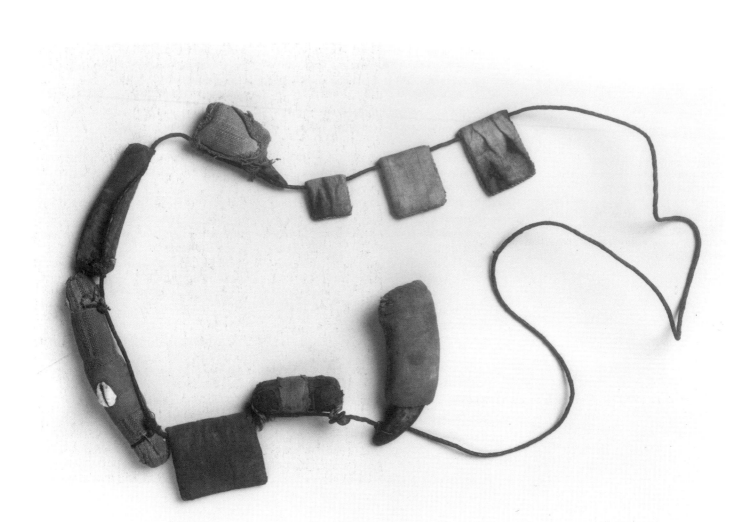

97
Necklace of nine charm
pendants
Cloth, leather and horn,
Mande, Gambia

93
Grape shot in bag
Lead, 18th century

133
Drum, 'The Nanda'
Paramacca tribe, Seeton Ponta Village, Marawyne River,
French Guyana

96
Log book of the UNITY, describing a revolt by slaves
on board
1769–71

165
Figure of an enslaved African breaking free of his chains
Carved wood, American, late 19th century

ery, others simply for their own rights. In the United States, for example, by the 1840s, free blacks such as Henry Bibb, William Wells Brown, Frederick Douglass, Lunsford Lane, Sojourner Truth, Harriet Tubman and Samuel R. Ward spoke to anti-slavery audiences throughout the north.

A first priority was to avoid being forced back into slavery. Many free African Americans, particularly women, pooled their resources in mutual aid and benevolent associations to protect themselves against destitution. For example, in Philadelphia in 1838, two thirds of the free black benevolent societies were exclusively female, including the Sisterly Union and the Daughters of Absalom. Each member would pay dues and if they fell ill or died they would be given aid or receive a decent burial and their children would be cared for.

A second priority was to abolish slavery. Though the abolitionists' movement was headed mainly by whites, who got most attention, its power and energy came from blacks. Both those that escaped from slavery and those born free supported the work and newspapers of the white abolitionists. For example, William Lloyd Garrison's *Liberator*, founded in 1831, was kept alive by black subscriptions which amounted to ninety per cent of all subscriptions in the first year. David Ruggles, a central figure in the 'Underground Railroad', helped keep up the paper's circulation.

Writing and publication were central to the activities of free black people. One of the most radical written demands for an end to slavery was published early in the nineteenth century. *Walker's Appeal, in Four Articles* by David Walker was most notable for its advocacy of armed rebellion against whites if they refused emancipation. There were others. For example, in 1827, the first black newspaper, *Freedom's Journal*, was started in New York, and was edited by Samuel Cornish and John Russwurm. The paper lasted only a few years, but many others followed it.

Free blacks were also prominent in the Underground Railroad and they played a major role in aiding runaways. Most 'conductors' (who led the runa-

ways) were themselves escaped slaves, who returned to aid others. Harriet Tubman is reported to have personally helped three hundred runaway slaves.

Free black people were active not only within their own nations, but also in establishing international links. Africans throughout the Diaspora travelled to oppose slavery and the oppression and exploitation of Africans. From the United States, activists and educators such as Martin Delany, Edward Wilmott Blydon, Sarah Remond Parker and Alexander Crummel travelled to England and across Europe. In eighteenth-century Britain the work of Olaudah Equiano, Ignatius Sancho and Ottobah Cuguano challenged slavery and the vilification of African societies.

Women's additional struggles

One of the major limitations of existing analyses of resistance is that they have largely ignored the role that women played in actively resisting as well as laying the foundations that enabled men to resist actively. For example, Bush maintains that 'because the woman was subjected to the same conditions as the male slave, she reacted to enslavement, punishment and coercion in similar ways, from everyday resistance to outright rebellion'.[4] Nor was it just the exploitation and domination of whites that black women had to endure. Bush argues persuasively that `the slave woman, subjected to both black and white patriarchy, in addition to experiencing class exploitation was also a victim of racism. It is in this framework of triple oppression that her achievements should be measured.'[5]

African women were most likely to resist by talking back to slave masters and overseers. They were also more likely to poison slave owners or contaminate their food. Many invoked mystic curses that were believed to be potent. As cooks and house servants, they were in a privileged position for poisoning and other acts of sabotage.

Free black women were active in a number of ways. Free African American women – including Harriet Tubman, Ellen Craft and Anna Murray Douglass – helped individual slaves gain their freedom, as well as working on the vigilance committees that pro-

PUNISHMENT RECORD BOOK of *Plantation Friendship*
of *Saint James, Island of Jamaica* and having a number of *Three*

Date of Entry.	Name of Slave.	Nature of Offence.	Time and Place of Punishment.

142
Punishment Records, Friendship Plantation
Jamaica, January-June 1828

vided runaway slaves with clothing, food, money and help in finding employment. The Colored Female Religious and Moral Society of Salem, Massachusetts, was formed in 1818, and the Female Anti-Slavery Society of Salem was formed in 1832 by African American women 'to promote the welfare of our colour'.

African American women in the abolition movement had to contend with the racism of many white abolitionist women who refused to allow black women to become members of their organizations.

Conclusion

Resistance to slavery is testimony to the indomitable will of the human spirit. As the numerous examples above demonstrate, Africans resisted in a multitude of ways, and for many different purposes. Some resisted every attempt to control their lives; others resisted day-to-day domination; others fought against certain excesses.

Though many Africans were murdered, and many others were psychologically smothered by white domination, the collective will of Africans refused to accept white domination. An understanding of resistance demonstrates the variety and vitality of the African spirit. European enslavement of Africans certainly victimised them; but it did not leave them with a victim mentality. Africans were not victims, but survivors.[6]

1. B. Martin and M. Spurrell (eds.), *The Journal of a Slave Trader - John Newton*, London 1962.

2. Angela Davis, *Women, Race and Class*, The Women's Press, 1981, p.21.

3. John Blassingame, *The Slave Community*, Oxford University Press, 1972, p.221.

4. Barbara Bush, *Slave Women in Caribbean Society, 1650-1838*, Heinemann Publishers, 1990, p.6.

5. *Ibid.*, p.8.

6. See also Theresa L. Amitt and Julie A. Mattei, *Race, Gender and Work*, Boston, South End Press, 1991; Barbara Christian, 'The Race for Theory', *Feminist Studies*, vol. 14, Spring 1988, pp.67-79; Paul Gilroy, *The Black Atlantic, Modernity and Double Consciousness*, London and New York, Verso, 1993; Leon Litwack, *Been in the Storm so Long*, Vintage Books, 1977; Orlando Patterson, *The Sociology of Slavery*, Granada Publishing, 1967.

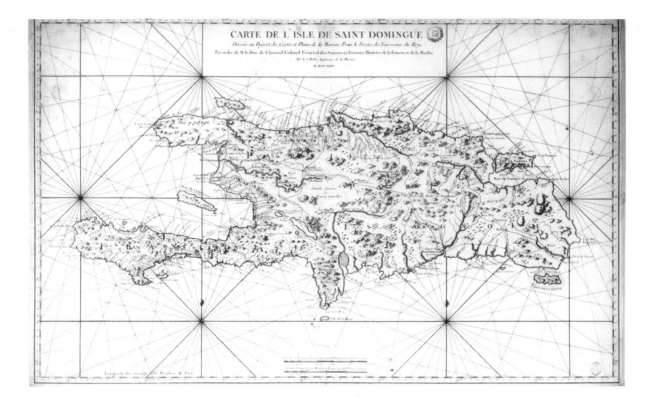

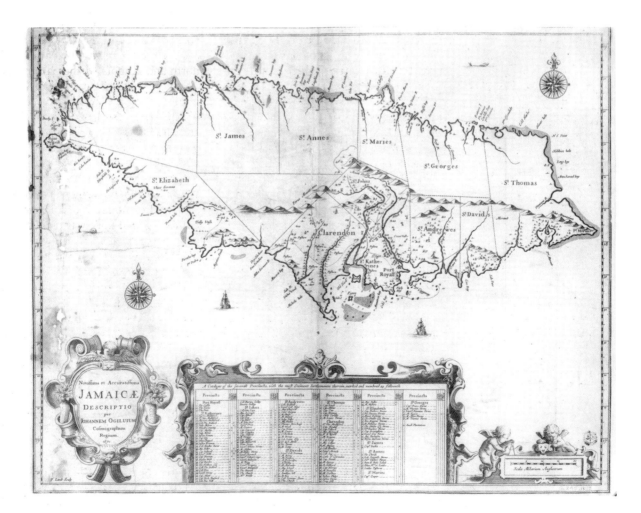

Caribbean Slave Society

ALISSANDRA CUMMINS

104
Map of St Domingue, printed chart
Jacques Nicolas Bellin, Paris, 1764

105
Map of Jamaica divided into parishes,
printed chart
John Ogilby, London, 1671

Within the context of West Indian history, slave society is almost synonymous with plantation society. The plantation system gave shape and structure to the ordering of relationships within the islands and put a special stamp on the history of the region. Firmly established during the seventeenth century, it lasted without significant alteration throughout the eighteenth century and continued in a modified form even after slaves were freed in the nineteenth century.

The plantation system was initially established as an economic enterprise geared towards deriving maximum benefits for the planters who owned and controlled it. The plantation and its correlative, slave labour, became the very essence of organized society in the Caribbean. The plantation maintained the balance of power and control within the existing political and social structures and preserved the economic imbalance amongst the various interest groups.

The plantation system defined an ideology of racism which developed and grew throughout the period of slavery. Its devastating effect is still entrenched in Caribbean society today – three hundred years of human existence translated into economic and political power for the planters, social and economic degradation for the slaves. Rigid stratification ensured the denigration of African cultural systems and the continuing degeneration of the African condition. The myth of white superiority and black dependence was nurtured by forced compliance to the dominant group.

The social structure was caste-like and was firmly supported by legal, political and social developments. There were basically three castes, the whites, the blacks and the coloureds. Due to the volume of the slave trade, the sugar planters were soon heavily outnumbered by their slaves. The black population surpassed the white one in Barbados around 1660, in Jamaica soon after 1670 and in the Leeward Islands soon after 1680. By 1713 there were four blacks to every white in the English colonies. However, the whites maintained their social, economic and political ascendancy through progressive subjugation by legal, military, cultural, material and economic means.

The peculiar nature of Caribbean slavery forces us 'to make a clear distinction between slavery as an abstract legal status and as an actual institution involving economic functions and interpersonal relationships'.[1] This definition of slavery created harsh realities for slaves.

Origins of Caribbean slaves

The sugar planters of Barbados, Jamaica and the Leeward Islands were the first Englishmen to practice slavery on a large scale. Before the close of the seventeenth century they had brought a quarter of a million Africans to the six Islands.

English slaving records from the late seventeenth century are useful in identifying the origins of Africans forced to migrate to the Caribbean. More than seventy per cent of the slaves imported by the Royal African Company from 1673 to 1689 came from the Guinea coasts, with the rest divided equally between the Senegambia region further north and Angola further south. Thus slaves in the Caribbean originated primarily from the Windward Coast (modern Liberia), the Gold Coast (Ghana), and the Slave Coast (Togoland, Dahomey and Western Nigeria).[2]

The English believed that the variety of languages and the intense tribal rivalries among the Guinea Coast peoples hindered enslaved blacks from 'combining' against their masters. A writer of 1694 recorded that the 'safety of the Plantation depends upon having Negroes from all parts of Guiny, who not understanding each other languages and customs, do not, and cannot agree to rebel, as they would do ... when there are too many Negroes from one country'.[3]

English planters were profoundly ignorant and contemptuous of West African cultures. They were satisfied to perpetuate prejudicial stereotypes: the view that Papaws from the Slave Coast were docile and agreeable; that Coromantees from the Gold Coast were proud, brave and rebellious; that Ibos from the Niger Delta were timorous and despondent. All of these were prefer-

116
One Penny Token, obverse: image of a
head 'I SERVE', reverse: image of a
pineapple, 'BARBADOES PENNY 1788'
Copper, Barbados, 1788

able to the Bantu-speaking Angolans who were reputed to be rebellious, bellicose and lazy into the bargain. Time and again the planters underestimated the tenacity of cultural ties. By the end of the eighteenth century most Caribbean slaves were creoles and only a small percentage were African born.

Daily life

For the vast majority of slaves, life was a long and monotonous routine involving heavy work in the field from 6.00 am to 6.00 pm. The principles and structure of work organization on a plantation created a distinct hierarchical structure not just between white and black but between the house slaves, the field slaves and the artisans. It was a system based not on merit but on age, proximity and sex, with the work gangs at the bottom of the structure and the household workers nearest their masters at the top.

Blacks were dependent for most of their necessities of food, clothing and shelter. On the plantation slaves were generally housed in a row of little oblong huts, built out of sticks and cane trash, facing on to a yard. Each hut was modestly furnished with a sleeping mat, a cooking pot and one or two calabash gourds cut to make cups or spoons. In town very few negroes were permitted inside their masters' houses but lived segregated in small huts behind.[4]

Health was also often related to status, and the rigours of field labour clearly had a negative effect on the longevity of these workers. The list of illnesses which pervaded the eighteenth- and nineteenth-century slave population included consumption, dysentery, dropsy, yaws, yellow fever, elephantiasis and tetanus. But most critical of all was malnutrition.[5] While some slave laws specified the basic food necessities, compliance was by no means universal. Dunn records that the slaves ate a monotonous, meagre and starchy diet of cassava, corn, plantain, beans and yams, supplemented by rum on Saturdays, and meat whenever an animal died of disease. In fact there is some evidence that planters underfed slaves in order to help break their resistance.

125
Auction hammer
Ivory with silver band, (?) 19th century

Fig.8
'Cutting sugar cane' from H T de la Beche, *Notes on Jamaica*, 1825
Sugar cultivation was very labour-intensive. Harvesting involved long hours of arduous, back-breaking work, by men, women and children.

Fig.9
'Shipping the sugar' from W Clark, *Ten Views of Antigua*, 1823
Antigua was one of the main sugar producing islands of the British West Indies.

Fig.10
Insurrection on board a slave ship
from W Fox, *Brief History*, 1851
Uprisings on board ship happened
regularly and were put down with
brutal ferocity.

188
Plate with scene of former slave
family in front of cabin, 'FREEDOM
FIRST OF AUGUST 1838'
White earthenware with blue transfer-
printing

113
24 Shilling Piece, silver
Danish West Indies, 1767

Slave laws – control of slaves

During the seventeenth century, sugar planters created one of the harshest systems of servitude in Western history, the repercussions of which continue to be felt as we move towards the twenty-first century. Lacking English precedents to draw upon, the colonists quickly adopted the system brought to the West Indies by the Spanish and worked up a legal code and a set of customs that divided island society starkly into two classes, white masters and black slaves.[6] The Negro was defined as a chattel and treated as a piece of conveyable property, without rights or redress in law. This differed starkly from older forms of bondage in classical antiquity because of its racist character. Slavery in the English islands was ruthlessly exploitative from the outset and nakedly racial – a device to maximise sugar production and as cheaply as possible.

Supposedly, the English did not at first distinguish in any meaningful way between white indentured servants and the Negroes who arrived from Africa. White and black labourers were equally unfree, the only real difference being that whites served for specified terms, and blacks served indefinitely. But this is surely not a valid interpretation given the immediate categorization of Africans as heathen brutes to be treated as chattels.[7]

While it is true that the English colonists initially avoided defining the nature of slavery, they worked out the problem pragmatically and built up piecemeal a regulatory structure governing their relations with slaves. In 1637 in Barbados the Government Council decreed that 'Negroes and Indians, that came here to be sold, should serve for life, unless a contract was before made to the contrary'. While this might apply to some of the Indians, no contracts seem to have been made with any Negroes.

The problem of interracial sex soon arose. In 1644 the Antigua assembly composed a law against miscegenation, forbidding 'caarnall coppullation between Christian and Heathen', the latter defined as Negroes and Indians. A freeman or free woman who fornicated

with a black was fined. A servant had his or her term of indenture extended. The offending heathen was branded or shipped. A mulatto child produced by a mixed union was enslaved until age eighteen or twenty-one (and in 1672 it was extended to life).[8]

Since the planters did not want to assimilate or acculturate such an alien population, they segregated themselves socially and culturally from the blacks to preserve their own identity. Thus to maintain control a system was devised to intimidate, police and discipline the slaves. The slave laws enacted by the island legislatures in the seventeenth century, therefore, tell us a good deal about the treatment of Negroes and the character of slavery in the Caribbean colonies.

By 1661 Barbados had a comprehensive slave code. The Act passed by the Barbados assembly 'for the better ordering and governing of Negroes' was the most important piece of legislation issued in the island in the seventeenth century. The preamble to this document assumes that Negro slaves are chattels for it undertakes 'to protect them as wee doe men's other goods and chattles'. It was re-enacted with slight modification by later Barbados assemblies in 1676, 1682 and 1688 and was copied by the Assemblies in Jamaica (1664), South Carolina (1696) and Antigua (1702).

In 1685 another law tried to shut down the Sunday markets by prohibiting white persons from trading with Negroes for pots of sugar and jars of molasses filled from their masters' pots. The slave laws legitimised a state of war between blacks and whites, sanctified rigid segregation and institutionalised an early warning system against slave revolts.

The slave code accorded masters, servants and slaves carefully differentiated rights and obligations, with the master being given almost total authority over his slaves and much less power over his servants.

Slaves' lives could be forfeited for relatively minor crimes and their bodies mutilated for even more minor transgressions. While slave conspiracies and uprisings abound as evidence of the blacks' unequal struggle, little is known of their attempts to control their

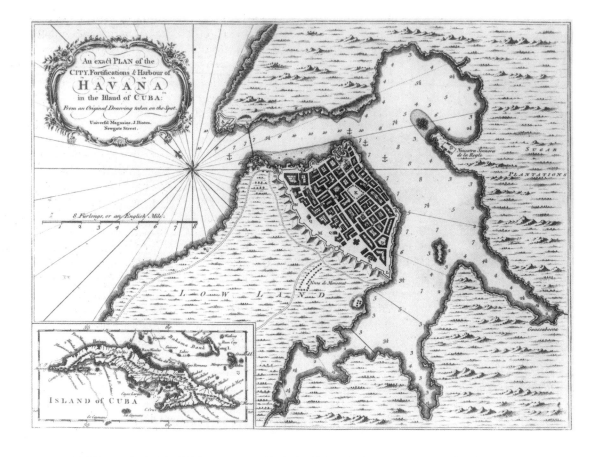

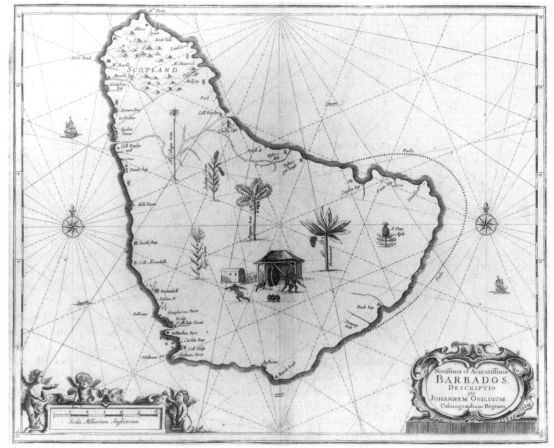

reality, through their day-to-day social and economic activities. By the eighteenth century, an elaborate and comprehensive superstructure had been established which confirmed indubitably the ideology of slaves as property. It is a rather exquisite irony that much of the emphasis of law-making from this period went into protecting the planters' property from themselves.

African-Caribbean culture

Caribbean culture is difficult to interpret in terms of its origins, and questions of identity and tradition continue to plague Caribbean people. The persistence of African cultural continuities in African-American and Caribbean societies has also been used to serve different, and opposite, ideological ends.

The violent uprooting of Africans from their homeland to enslavement certainly took its toll on the integrity of African culture in the Caribbean. Although the Africans brought a set of systems – socio-hierarchical kinship, beliefs, languages – to the Caribbean many of them were almost destroyed by slavery. The uneven distribution of power and lack of contact with home cultures meant that Africans had to undergo drastic cultural accommodation – acculturation.[9]

Slaves brought to the Caribbean from the West sub-Saharan African region (Senegal to Angola) emerged from an area of great ethnic diversity. Nevertheless there is an underlying unity in a number of shared cultural features.

Despite the large number of African languages used within the West and Central regions there was a linguistic unity within the area and slaves in the Caribbean who came from different ethnic groups were able to communicate with each other. While there was great diversity in the words of the various languages and dialects used, there was a general similarity in the grammar used. Caribbean languages have retained a number of African words in modern use. However, the main African influences lie in the language systems. Also the sentence structure, pitch tone, the combination of sound (e.g. suck teeth) and gesture (e.g. cut-eye), an open syllable structure, all have their origins in African language systems. A major feature of linguistic transfer from Africa to the Caribbean is the proverb, highlighting a pervasive African world view and philosophy, as well as a simple way of putting things that is typical of that area.[10]

Finally in the Caribbean there evolved several common creole patois, comprising European and African elements, which ensured communication amongst the slaves.

As a general rule Caribbean languages are not seen as belonging to the African tradition but are judged against Greco-Roman norms of language structure: for example, inflections are regarded as the essential part of the ideal language structure. Creole languages tend, therefore, to be negatively evaluated in relation to these norms. Those which have managed to escape this stigma have progressed (or are progressing) to the status of official and national languages (e.g. Papiamentu) and are positive symbols of national identity.

African religious beliefs were also assimilated into the culture. The Asante-derived religion of the maroons of Surinam and Jamaica recognised Dahomean and Bantu deities and the Dahomean religion of Haiti contains Yoruba deities. The tradition of religious syncretism (fusion of African and Christian religions) is typical in the creole religious forms of Shango, Vaudun, Punkumina and Santeria. In Jamaica, for example, the Asante-based religion of the maroons and Kumina, based on the Bantu religion, have given way to Pukumina with its observance of both Christian and African deities. After this came Revivalism, which preserved ancestor veneration and spirit possession. Certain Caribbean religious forms such as spirit possession have been assigned an African frame of reference.[11]

Indigenous economic systems in the Caribbean were much influenced by the West African traditions of credits and marketing. Thus traditional Southern Nigerian rotating credit and savings associations, termed the *esusu* (Yoruba) or the *isusu* (Igbo), were also established in the islands where they were known as 'the hand' and 'pardners', or regionally as 'susu'. They still remain

103
Plan of Havana, with inset map of Cuba
John Hinton, from the *Universal Magazine*, London, c.1762

Fig.11
Map of Barbados, by John Ogilvy, London, mid-17th century
This map includes drawings of a sugar press and crops such as sugar cane, pawpaw and pineapple.

Fig. 12
'Cutting sugar cane' from W. Clark, *Ten Views in Antigua*, 1823

in use today. Higgling and peddling formed the backbone of the islands' internal marketing system, based on West African forms of bartering produce for goods. These systems, which were adapted by enslaved Africans throughout the Diaspora, have now developed into an intricate regional network.

Games, too, have played an important socialising role in the community. Found all over Africa, the popular game 'mankala' or 'warri' (*owari*) in West Africa made its way to the Caribbean and became part of the African cultural legacy of the region. The game is a challenge to dexterity, calculation, anticipation and artistry. Traditionally played only by men (or in a few cases by women of superior status) 'warri' was played in public and involves great audience participation. For the Bush Negroes in Surinam, warri was not simply a game but maintained many of the customary patterns and social etiquettes associated with it in Africa. In Barbados and Trinidad, for example, the game was often played as part of a wake for the dead.

Caribbean folk-tales, Anansi stories or stories featuring a spider and other animals existed in the pre-slavery culture of slaves. They expressed a morality which the Africans brought with them and, more importantly, they form part of the African narrative and performance traditions which were important parts of African communal interaction that helped mould new African-Caribbean communities.

1. D. B. Davis, *The Problems of Slavery in Western Cultures*, New York 1966, p.25.

2. For a more detailed analysis of the volume of the slave trade see P. D. Curtin, *The Atlantic Slave Trade: A Census*, Madison 1969, pp.122-23, 128-30.

3. An excellent reference work on slave origins is R. S. Dunn, *Sugar and Slaves: The rise of the planter class in the West Indies, 1624-1713*, London 1973, esp. pp.229-38. See also K. G. Davies, *The Royal African Company*, pp.213-33.

4. Early slave life has been described in detail in R. Ligon, *A True and Exact History of the Island of Barbados*, London 1657. Hans Sloane, *A Voyage to the Islands of Madera, Barbados, Nieves, S. Christophers and Jamaica*, London 1707-25, is similarly useful, if somewhat ethnocentric in its observations.

5. K. F. Kiple, *The Caribbean Slave: A Biological History*, Cambridge 1984, pp.76-103, offers fascinating insights into the effects of disease and sickness on the survival of enslaved Africans.

6. E. V. Goveia, *Slave Society in the British Leeward Islands*, Yale, 1965, pp.152-202, still remains the acknowledged authority on this topic.

7. Dunn, *op. cit.*, p.227.

8. Leeward Islands MSS Laws, 1644-1673, C.O. 154/1/49-51.

9. Aspects of the African Caribbean cultural experience have been analysed in depth in G. K. Lewis, *The Growth of the Modern West Indies*, New York and London 1968, pp.30-54.

10. Valuable sources on the development of Caribbean languages include M. Alleyne, *Root of Jamaican Culture*, London, Pluto Press, 1988.

11. R. F. Thompson, *Flash of the Spirit: African and Afro-American Art and Philosophy*, New York 1983, pp.16-31, 163-179, offers a valuable insight into the origins of existing forms of religious syncretism in the Caribbean.

Women in Slavery and the Transatlantic Slave Trade

JENNIFER LYLE MORGAN

The transatlantic slave trade was a human atrocity that has yet to be duplicated. The millions of men and women transported from sub-Saharan Africa, as well as those left behind, experienced a degree of dislocation, grief and cultural devastation that is difficult for contemporary researchers, readers or museum-goers to comprehend.

Our understanding of the trade and its consequences is still being refined. Like many historical events, many of our images of the trade are incomplete or, indeed, misleading. Erroneous impressions of enslaved Africans – snatched by strangers, bereft of spirit or culture, incapable of resisting their enslavement – have become part of our inherited vision. These impressions bar a more complex and accurate understanding of the slave trade and its significance for those men and women who were enslaved.

Understanding the particular experience of enslaved women in the slave trade is especially important. As a minority of the total number of the enslaved, women's experience in slavery and the slave trade has largely been disregarded. At best, historians have assumed that the generic term 'slave' encompassed both men and women. However, the particular experiences of African women and their female descendants had particular consequences upon the experience of enslavement – both for themselves and for their male counterparts. Women's access to particular components of their African society's culture, their agricultural work, and their sexual and reproductive identities are just three of the elements that we must look toward in order to assess the impact of the transatlantic slave trade fully.

Many European observers of West and West Central Africa commented upon the industry of African women. They saw them as constant workers, some even characterizing these women as drudges or 'slaves'. While these observations are coloured by the Eurocentric perspective of the observers, they are, nonetheless, important windows into the lives of African women and men prior to and during the disruption caused by the transatlantic slave trade. Jean Barbot, one of the more frequent European travellers to visit Africa, was quite struck by the place of women in the societies he encountered. He noted that women were the primary agricultural workers, as well as the household member responsible for cooking and child-rearing. Barbot was often confused by African behaviour, particularly when it did not correspond to 'proper' male and female conduct. He found it difficult to understand the role that men played in society, and fell back upon the simplistic formulation that they did nothing, and were examples of the 'laziness' of 'Africans'. When approached by traders on one of his voyages, Barbot saw the group of men and women approaching his ship as 'traders and their wives' – clearly it was outside his realm of possibility that the women were traders in their own right. As the primary producers of some manufactured goods – thread and cloth, for example – it is conceivable that women would have, rightly, been at the forefront of trading and economic exchanges with the newly arriving Europeans. This despite English visitors' inability to understand social behaviour unfamiliar to them.[1]

European traders were similarly troubled by the freedom with which African women approached them. Many Europeans ascribed licentiousness and sexual immorality to African women. The independence that characterized some African women's lives, as well as their relative state of undress in comparison with the women with which European men were familiar, led to assumptions that African men and women lived in a loose and ungoverned state. Sexuality, and its corollary chastity, acted as symbols of civilization as far as European observers were concerned. As they assessed African women's sexuality, they drew conclusions about African humanity that would have very important consequences – most important being the widespread acceptance that African people deserved mass enslavement at the hands of European colonists.

As previously mentioned, African men and women were not enslaved in equal numbers. The majority of those enslaved by all European nations throughout the period of the transatlan-

11
Carving of a woman and child
Carved and painted wood, Lualli River, Cacongo, West Central Africa, 19th century

tic slave trade were men. One might assume that women were not as highly valued as labourers by Europeans who believed that women were weaker and poorer workers; that the basis for the imbalance was located in European attitudes and assumptions. However, those women who were enslaved in the Americas were never 'protected' by European owners from hard labour; they were exploited in the sugar, rice and cotton fields. The explanation why women were not enslaved by Europeans in the same numbers as their male counterparts is found in Africa. The central position that African women occupied in their own societies as agricultural and craft producers meant that, from the onset, there were fewer women available to European purchasers. But there were very few women who were not forced to labour somewhere; many women were enslaved on the African continent or sold into the Occidental slave trade. Most slaves in Africa were, in fact, women; a testament to women's importance as labourers. Those Africans sold on the transatlantic slave trade were the men and women who were not highly valued, for whatever reason, by the men and women who made them available to European purchasers.[2]

The gendered nature of the transatlantic slave trade had very important consequences for those women and men who were not enslaved by Europeans. In African societies up and down the west coast of the continent, social relations and interactions were invariably altered as more and more men were taken from their shores. Over the course of the seventeenth and eighteenth centuries women became the significant majority of some African societies, outnumbering men by as much as two to one. At the same time, the number of women enslaved in Africa increased. Nonetheless, in a crucial departure from women's experience in the Americas, many slave women in African societies were integrated into slave-owning families as 'junior co-wives'. The children born of these marriages were evidence of women's social mobility. One can only speculate how men and women's lives in African societies were altered on a

19
Calabash
With inscribed geometrical patterns, Rabba, Nigeria, 1860

20
Calabash
Painted with geometrical designs in red and black, Garoua, Cameroon

day-to-day basis as a result of these shifts in gender ratios. But one must assume that the reverberations encompassed almost all aspects of society – work, culture and family life.[3]

It is true that those men and women who remained on the African continent suffered consequences of the transatlantic slave trade, but certainly their sufferings paled in comparison to those who were transported from their ancestral home to a new life of strange lands, strange peoples and forced labour. Even before their arrival in the Americas, enslaved Africans endured the Middle Passage – a period in which one's sense of future was wrenched away as one bore an interminable wait.

Once African men and women arrived at the coast, they were confined in fortresses and castles until the arrival of ships from Europe that would take them to the Americas. So-called 'castle working slaves' were obtained for the fortresses. The Royal African Company stipulated that these be half women and half men. At these fortresses women were subjected to the sexual demands of the white men who were stationed there to oversee the business of enslavement. These factors, as they were called, required enslaved women to clean and cook for them, as well as to submit to sexual advances. The only thing that could work in the favour of these women was that they were subjected to a stable situation which could ultimately provide them with means to escape or manoeuvre. Other women and men, however, were not held at fortresses but were sold in small numbers to ships that would make their way slowly along a river coastline. This method could mean, for those amongst the first to be enslaved, weeks on board a ship before setting out on open sea. In this situation as well, women were particularly vulnerable to exploitation and assault on the part of European sailors anxious to give vent to their sexual appetites.[4]

Once a loaded slave ship left the African coast, the seven to eight week journey to the Americas began. On many ships, women were allowed a limited degree of freedom that was denied to enslaved men. While men were confined to the hold of the ship at almost all times, women were often allowed to remain above decks, sometimes without the shackles which bound the men day and night. The women's relative freedom of mobility allowed them to move about and communicate with one another in a fashion which men could not. In some cases, as on board the *Amistad* in 1839, women took advantage of that freedom to plan revolts or attacks upon the white sailors who enslaved them. For most women, however, time above deck meant unwanted exposure. It subjected them to rape and attack from sailors. Some women were impregnated by sailors during the journey. Others, whose misfortune it was to give birth on board, saw their infants thrown into the sea since they were too young to bring a good price at the auction block. For many women, the Middle Passage – a time of unspeakable horror and degradation for all enslaved Africans – was a period of sexual brutalisation that could have only served as a bleak foreshadowing of what was to come.[5]

Once a slave ship arrived at its destination the enslaved women and men were 'cleaned up' and put on display for potential buyers. Slave purchasers often complained that ships arrived with their 'human cargoes' badly diseased and damaged. Much of that sickness was the result of inadequate food and water during the Middle Passage, as well as the diseases which were the inevitable result of the human excrement that was allowed to build up in the holds of the slave ships. Potential purchasers of these women and men therefore felt it their right to examine their 'property' intimately, subjecting the enslaved to an excruciating violation of their bodies. At this moment, one would imagine, the sexual violation that had been the sole fate of many women, both prior to and during the journey, became somewhat universal.

After being purchased and surviving the 'seasoning' period, during which those enslaved women and men who did not die had time to adapt to their new environment, the newly enslaved would be put to work.

Although life in the Americas for the enslaved is primarily understood through this lens of work, other impor-

12
Carving of a woman in a cloth skirt
Carved and painted wood, with (?)printed cotton skirt, Winneba, Ghana, 19th century

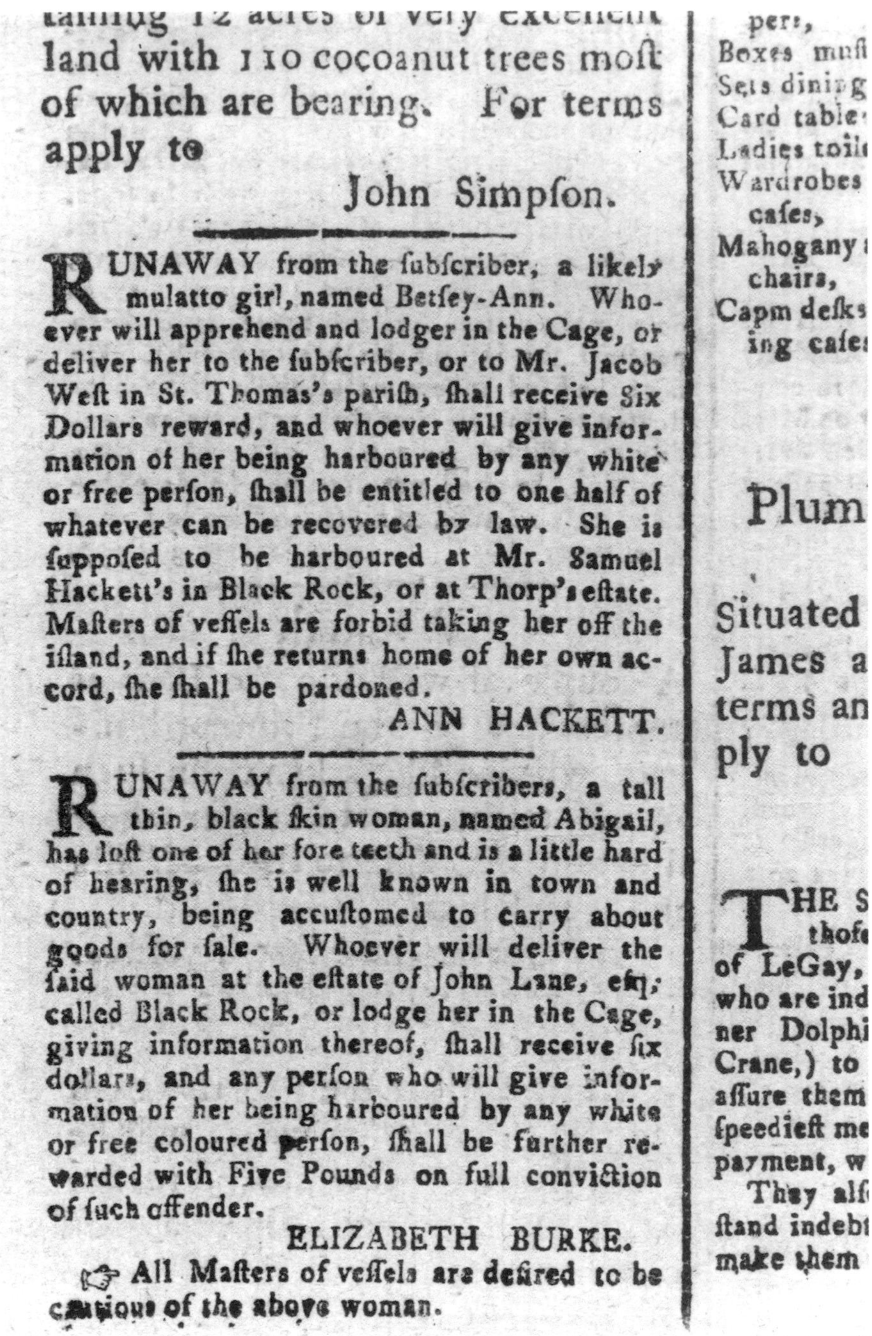

taining 12 acres of very excellent land with 110 cocoanut trees moſt of which are bearing. For terms apply to

John Simpſon.

RUNAWAY from the ſubſcriber, a likely mulatto girl, named Betſey-Ann. Whoever will apprehend and lodger in the Cage, or deliver her to the ſubſcriber, or to Mr. Jacob Weſt in St. Thomas's pariſh, ſhall receive Six Dollars reward, and whoever will give information of her being harboured by any white or free perſon, ſhall be entitled to one half of whatever can be recovered by law. She is ſuppoſed to be harboured at Mr. Samuel Hackett's in Black Rock, or at Thorp's eſtate. Maſters of veſſels are forbid taking her off the iſland, and if ſhe returns home of her own accord, ſhe ſhall be pardoned.

ANN HACKETT.

RUNAWAY from the ſubſcribers, a tall thin, black ſkin woman, named Abigail, has loſt one of her fore teeth and is a little hard of hearing, ſhe is well known in town and country, being accuſtomed to carry about goods for ſale. Whoever will deliver the ſaid woman at the eſtate of John Lane, eſq; called Black Rock, or lodge her in the Cage, giving information thereof, ſhall receive ſix dollars, and any perſon who will give information of her being harboured by any white or free coloured perſon, ſhall be further rewarded with Five Pounds on full conviction of ſuch offender.

ELIZABETH BURKE.

☞ All Maſters of veſſels are deſired to be cautious of the above woman.

pers,
Boxes muſ
Sets dinin
Card table
Ladies toil
Wardrobes
cafes,
Mahogany
chairs,
Capm deſks
ing caſe

Plum

Situated
James a
terms an
ply to

THE S
thoſe
of LeGay,
who are ind
ner Dolphi
Crane,) to
aſſure them
ſpeedieſt me
payment, w
They alſ
ſtand indebt
make them

Fig. 13
Advertisement for runaways, from *Barbados Mercury*, Saturday 7 January 1797
Slaves regularly ran away from their owners, many to the maroon communities which existed in all parts of the Americas.

tant components affected the communities in which enslaved men and women lived. One of those components was simply the inability to create lives with one another. Until the mid-eighteenth century in North America, slave societies could not reproduce themselves, because of low birth rates, high infant mortality, and the exorbitant toll of disease. Newly enslaved Africans had continually to be added to existing populations in order to maintain their numbers. In the period directly preceding the American War of Independence,for the first time the influx of new Africans was no longer necessary in the Southern colonies; babies were born and were surviving to adulthood.[6]

Clearly, one of the most important factors in the ability of a population to reproduce itself is the number of women. In most Caribbean slave societies it was not until the nineteenth century, in some cases not until after slavery had been abolished, that this reproduction was possible. Consequently, the entire cultural life of a slave society was linked to the presence or absence of women. In those areas, like the West Indies, where women were relatively absent and where there was a constant stream of newly enslaved African arrivals, religious and cultural links to African societies remained tangibly evident well into the nineteenth and twentieth centuries. In areas like the Southern North American colonies, however, where women's presence was more significant, African cultural forms became less decisive as a distinctly African-American, or creole, culture developed. This creolisation of culture was also accompanied by a particular agony. In the colonies of Maryland, Virginia, North Carolina, South Carolina and Georgia, there developed in the late eighteenth and early nineteenth century an internal slave trade that had terrible consequences for the enslaved. These states began to supply the states of the lower South – Alabama, Mississippi, Louisiana, Florida, Texas – with slaves born in the upper South. Parents and children were wrenched apart and families devastated as slave-owners profited from the demand for slaves that they were now able to fill.

Plainly, the nature of slavery in the

Americas varied considerably over time and space. This was true in the realm of work as well as in terms of reproduction and its consequences. The lives of enslaved Africans taken to Mexico in the sixteenth century, Jamaica in the seventeenth century, Virginia in the eighteenth century or Cuba in the nineteenth century were extraordinarily different from one another. Enslavement was not a static experience. It made a significant difference whether one was enslaved in a Mexican silver mine, on a Pennsylvanian ship, or on a South Carolina rice plantation.

Nevertheless, in terms of work, slavery for women did sustain a certain static quality. Enslaved women's lives in the Americas were characterized, above all, by incessant work. Slave societies developed around the production of export crops: the West Indies produced sugar and coffee, the Chesapeake produced tobacco, the American South produced cotton and rice. However, it is not the case that all slaves in Virginia, for example, were picking and growing tobacco. As a slave society developed there were roads and bridges to be built, bricks to be made, houses and buildings to be constructed, cattle to be tended, horses to be shoed, clothes to be sewn, boats to be loaded and ships to be sailed. Most of these jobs were done by enslaved Africans; none of them was done by women. Those who escaped field work, with the exception of a small number of domestic workers, were all men. So while some men could elude the monotony and hardship of the field, almost all women were required to spend their working lives cutting, gathering and stacking sugar cane, wading ankle deep in rice fields, or bent over cotton bolls.[7]

Ironically, the innovation that made these crops successful in the Americas came from the knowledge and experience brought by women. The agricultural skills which most African women brought with them to the Americas were, whether consciously or not, manipulated by white slave-owners. All the crops, with the exception of sugar, developed in the Americas by planters anxious for profit were ones commonly cultivated on the West Afri-

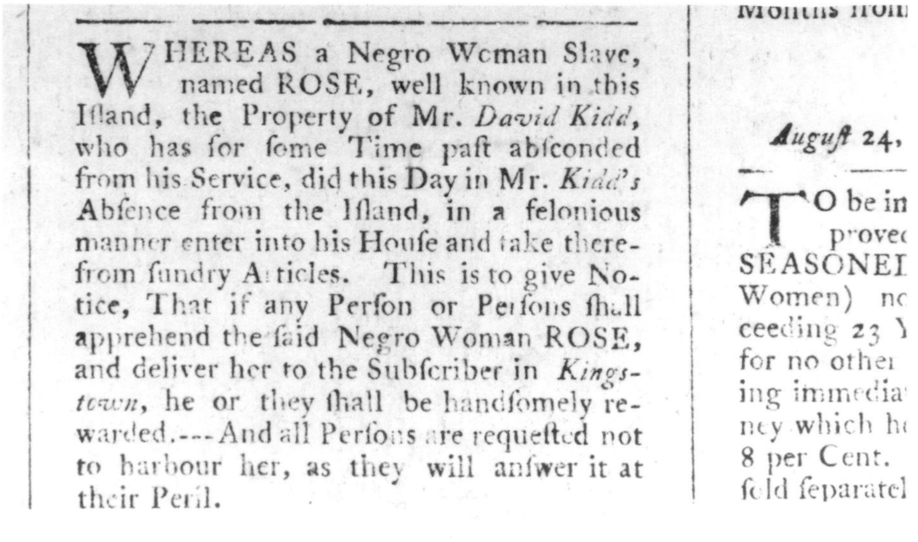

WHEREAS a Negro Woman Slave, named ROSE, well known in this Iſland, the Property of Mr. *David Kidd*, who has for ſome Time paſt abſconded from his Service, did this Day in Mr. *Kidd's* Abſence from the Iſland, in a felonious manner enter into his Houſe and take therefrom ſundry Articles. This is to give Notice, That if any Perſon or Perſons ſhall apprehend the ſaid Negro Woman ROSE, and deliver her to the Subſcriber in *Kingstown*, he or they ſhall be handſomely rewarded.---And all Perſons are requeſted not to harbour her, as they will anſwer it at their Peril.

Fig.14
Advertisement for a runaway female slave, from *The Royal St Vincent Gazette and General Advertiser,* Saturday 10 October 1789
Women generally ran away for short periods and feature less frequently in runaway advertisements.

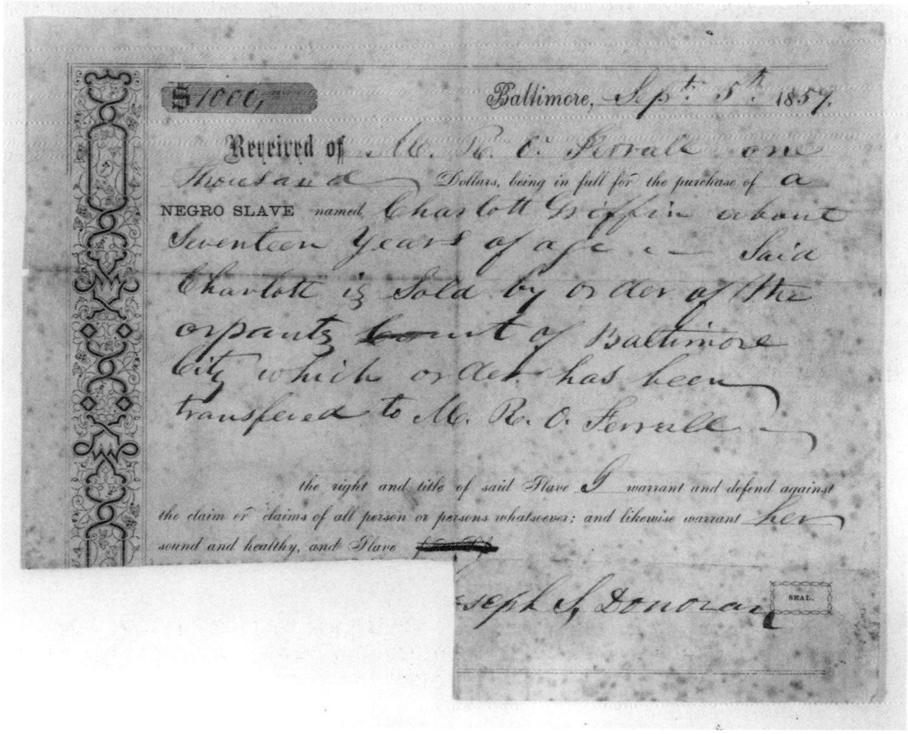

$1000/

Baltimore, Sept. 5th 1857

Received of Mr. R. O Ferrall one thousand Dollars, being in full for the purchase of a NEGRO SLAVE named Charlott Griffin about Seventeen years of age — Said Charlott is sold by order of the orphants ~~Court~~ of Baltimore City which order has been transfered to Mr. R. O Ferrall —

the right and title of said Slave I warrant and defend against the claim or claims of all person or persons whatsoever; and likewise warrant her sound and healthy, and Slave

Joseph G Donovan [SEAL.]

143
Receipt from Court of Baltimore to Mr R O'Ferrale for payment of $1000 for female slaves
Baltimore, 5 September 1859

can coast. Indigo, tobacco and rice, to name a few, were crops with which African women were far more experienced than European men. Enslaved men brought different skills. White colonists in South Carolina, for example, learned cattle-raising techniques from African men. Women's past role as agricultural workers prepared them for the work of the fields. One can only assume that for enslaved men the indignity of enslavement was intensified by being forced to do what, at home, was categorized as women's work.[8]

The household work – cooking, serving, child-tending – traditionally associated with female slaves was not the lot of most women during most of the period of slavery. The Caribbean, for example, was a place to which planters came without their families, intending to become rich and leave – if they came at all. Many simply hired a man to oversee the running of a plantation in their absence; there were few households that required 'staff'. It was not until the nineteenth century that white planters in many parts of the Americas turned their attention to the social niceties that came with acquired wealth and stability. As white society developed and domestic servants were needed, the chance to leave the field may have been welcomed by some enslaved women. Others, however, may have felt that the proximity to whites that came with domestic duties was distasteful or dangerous or both. Many enslaved domestic servants found themselves on duty for twenty-four hours a day, sleeping on the floor outside the doors of their owners, and only rarely seeing their own family. Cooks were sometimes fitted with masks to prevent them from eating from the kitchen; those who were not so fitted were supervised by whites convinced that all blacks were thieves and dishonest. The paranoia of slave-owners meant that domestic servants were constantly accused of poisoning or plotting to kill their owners. In some instances, those accusations were real. The proximity of domestic slaves to owners meant they were in the prime position to initiate revolt or rebellion. In other cases slave-owners were simply venting their generalised fear by falsely punishing the individual slaves

Fig.15
'A Female Negro Slave, with a Weight chained to her Ankle', from J G Stedman, *Narrative of a five year expedition against the Revolted Negroes of Surinam, 1772-77*, London, 1796
Means of restraint were frequently cumbersome and cruel.

141
Letter to Thomas Eaton, Swansea, from his slave, Pheba
Kingston, Jamaica, 12 March 1793

with whom they came in closest contact.

The close contact between owner and slave brought with it some very complex relationships. For example, slave women were routinely employed as wet nurses, or 'Mammies' for the white children who would grow to own them. High infant mortality among the enslaved meant that an enslaved woman would be given no time to grieve over the death of her infant before she was forced to put a white infant to her breast. It is difficult to imagine the tangle of resentment and tenderness felt by a woman in this position.[9]

Similarly complicated was the existence of sexual relationships between enslaved women and slave-owners. Some women were victims of rape, exposed to the unwanted and relentless sexual demands of men who wielded unchecked power over them. On the other hand, some used longer-term sexual relationships with slave-owners as a means towards obtaining better living conditions for themselves and their families, always aware of the fact that

the relationship's future was entirely out of their hands. Although real affection between slave and slave-owner could exist, it was often overshadowed by the realities of power. Women who found themselves in the role of 'mammy' or 'mistress' were women whose emotional lives were manipulated by slave-owners. They were expected to nurture those who owned them. They were expected to be loyal, loving and sexually available. They were expected to put the needs of their owner and his or her family before those of their own. When they submitted to the expectations of slave-owners they did so under force. Some women probably came to identify their own needs with those of their owners. Others resisted that identification and maintained an independent sense of identity and community. Neither endured the relationship without acquiring scars – physical or psychological.

There is no question that personal relationships between owners and slaves existed. Evidence for them can be found in the population of enslaved women and men who were freed or 'manumitted'. Despite being significantly outnumbered by men in the slave community, in the freed population women equalled, if not outnumbered, men. Women were manumitted in greater numbers than men throughout North America. Freed populations in North America were disproportionately female. Enslaved women were freed as a result of their association with slave-owners, or when female children, who were manumitted at a rate higher than male children, were freed with their mothers. This is not to say that the freed populations were born only of sexual relationships. Male and female domestic servants were manumitted for long service and 'loyalty'. In most slave societies, some slaves were manumitted for performing military services – although, clearly, these were always men. Likewise, slaves could purchase their freedom with money made from hiring their services out. An artisan would pay a fee to his owner for the privilege of working outside the plantation; he could then save his remaining wages to purchase himself out of slavery. Nonetheless, like those who served in the military, those who had skills to be hired out were, in all likelihood, male. It was therefore only in those societies in which slaves were allowed to purchase their freedom, or where there were substantial numbers of military conflicts, that the freed population was more equally balanced between male and female.[10]

Manumission was not simply a benevolent impulse. By manumitting a domestic servant or long-time labourer, a slave-owner abrogated his responsibility to care for an aged or disabled slave, male or female, who could no longer work. By allowing some slaves to purchase their freedom, slave-owners provided a controlled outlet, something to strive for, that instilled determined hard work among some of the enslaved. By rewarding military service, slave-owners encouraged the enslaved to identify themselves with those who owned them; uniting slave and slave-owners against a 'common' enemy.

Manumission was not, however, a common experience. Most enslaved women and men lived their entire lives without hope of obtaining their freedom. This did not stop many from attempting to take freedom for themselves. The parameters of enslavement for women – the decreased mobility in contrast to men, the lack of variety in their work, the proximity to slave-owners when doing domestic labour – shaped the form of resistance which most women chose. There were few full-scale slave rebellions in the American South, and among those that did occur women were rarely in the forefront. The revolutionary efforts of the Stono Rebellion in colonial South Carolina, the nineteenth-century struggles of Denmark Vesey in Louisiana or Nat Turner in Virginia were planned and executed by enslaved men whose mobility allowed them to traverse communities spreading information and conferring on strategy. When examining the resistance patterns of enslaved women, one finds women combatting slavery on more individual ground. In their capacity as domestics, women's most extreme form of revolt was the murder, most often through poison, of slaveholders. Less extreme forms of resistance included work slow-downs, the theft of food to feed themselves and their families, and the refusal to perform certain tasks. Resistance also took the form of running away. For women, who often had familial ties that dictated their ability to disappear completely, running away was often cyclical. A woman would disappear for a week or so, after which time she would return having illustrated to the slaveholder her ability to fly in the face of his or her orders. Men, who were less likely to have intimate family ties as a result of their majority presence in slave communities, were more likely to absent themselves on a permanent basis. Slaveholders who were faced with what they saw as a permanent attempt to run away would place advertisements in the local newspapers describing their absent 'property'. In colonial South Carolina, for example, the only women who appear in these advertisements are those who have run away with a man and children or in family groups.[11]

In slave societies in Latin America and the Caribbean, a form of resistance

192
Token, obverse:'Am I not a woman and a sister 1838', reverse: a kneeling woman, 'United States of America Liberty 1838' United States of America, 1838

known as 'marronage' was far more common than in the American South. Runaway slaves would come together in geographically isolated regions to form maroon societies – Africans and their descendants who lived, often in battle with white soldiers and slave-owners attempting to destroy them, independently. As it happened, marronage also took place in societies in which women were vastly outnumbered by men. Nevertheless, records of these communities are replete with mention of women and children, suggesting that women were particularly eager to create a space in which it was possibly to live, and raise children, freely.[12]

Ultimately, of course, the battles that enslaved women and men fought to obtain individual or collective freedom were successful. There are a few women whose names are still evident in the historical record: Nanny, the eighteenth-century Jamaican maroon leader, Sojourner Truth, the former slave who obtained her freedom and spoke widely on the evils of slavery during the struggle for abolition, and Harriet Tubman, who made over three hundred trips from the American South to the North, leading countless slaves to freedom. These women, however, are exceptional; most enslaved women and men remain nameless. As these individuals struggled to create stable lives and communities in the aftermath of enslavement, their experiences continued to be shaped by the particulars of gender. There are those who have argued that, in the Caribbean, women actually experienced a reduction in mobility and economic independence as formerly enslaved women and men embraced the European conventions of male and female behaviour during slavery's aftermath. Regardless of the truth of that claim, it is true that one of the defining symbols of freedom was the ability for African-American and Caribbean women to work in their own homes, providing the care and sustenance for their families that was denied them during enslavement. As it is during enslavement, so in the aftermath of slavery the particular experience of women is a central key to understanding slavery's impact upon the African-American and Caribbean communities.[13]

1. See John Barbot, *A Description of the Coasts of North and South Guinea ...* in A. Churchill (ed.), *A Collection of Voyages ...*, London, 1732; and Claire Robertson and Martin Klein (eds.), *Women and Slavery in Africa*, Wisconsin, University of Wisconsin Press, 1983.

2. See Herbert Klein, 'African Women in the Atlantic Slave Trade', in Robertson and Klein, *Women and Slavery in Africa*, pp.29-38.

3. See John Thornton, 'Sexual Demography: The Impact of the Slave Trade on Family Structure', in *Women and Slavery in Africa*, 39-48; Susan Herlin Broadhead, 'Slave Wives, Free Sisters: Bakongo Women and Slavery c.1700-1850', in *Women and Slavery in Africa*, pp.160-184; and Robin Law, *The Slave Coast of West Africa, 1550-1750; The Impact of the Atlantic Slave Trade on an African Society*, Oxford, Oxford University Press, 1981; Joseph Miller, *Way of Death: Merchant Capitalism and the Angolan Slave Trade, 1730-1830*, Madison, University of Wisconsin Press, 1988.

4. See Records of the Royal African Company, T70 series, Public Record Office, London.

5. See Howard Jones, *Mutiny on the Amistad; the Saga of a Slave Revolt and its Impact on American Abolition, Law, and Diplomacy*, New York and London, Oxford University Press, 1987; Colin Palmer, *Human Cargoes: The British Slave Trade to Spanish America, 1700-1739*, Urbana, University of Illinois Press, 1981; James Rawley, *The Transatlantic Slave Trade: A History*, New York, W.W. Norton & Company, 1981.

6. See Allan Kulikoff, *Tobacco and Slaves; The Development of Southern Cultures in the Chesapeake, 1680-1800*, especially 'Black Society', pp.317-436, Chapel Hill, University of North Carolina Press, 1986.

7. See Jacqueline Jones, *Labor of Love, Labor of Sorrow; Black Women, Work, and the Family, from Slavery to the Present*, New York, Basic Books, 1985.

8. See Daniel Littlefield, *Rice and Slaves: Ethnicity and the Slave Trade in Colonial South Carolina*, Chapter 4, 'Rice Cultivation and the Slave Trade', pp.74-114, Baton Rouge and London, Louisiana State University Press, 1981; and Peter H. Wood, *Black Majority: Negroes in Colonial South Carolina from 1670 through the Stono Rebellion*, Chapter 4, 'Black Pioneers', pp.95-130, New York, Knopf, 1974.

9. See Barbara Bush, *Slave Women in Caribbean Society 1650-1838*, Chapter 2, '"The Eye of the Beholder': Contemporary European Images of Black Women', pp.11-22, London, James Currey, 1990. Deborah Gray White, *Ar'n't I a Woman? Female Slaves in the Plantation South*, Chapter 1, 'Jezebel and Mammy: The Mythology of Female Slavery', pp.27-61, New York, W.W. Norton, 1985.

10. See Ira Berlin, *Slaves Without Masters; The Free Negro in the Antebellum South*, especially Part 1, 'The Emergence of the Free Negro Caste, 1775-1812', pp.15-134, New York, Vintage Books, 1976; and David Cohen and Jack Greene (eds.), *Neither Slave Nor Free: The Freedman of African Descent in the Slave Societies of the New World*, Baltimore, The Johns Hopkins University Press, 1972.

11. See Deborah Gray White, *Ar'n't I a Woman?*, especially Chapter 2, 'the Nature of Female Slavery', pp.62-90; Barbara Bush, *Slave Women in Caribbean Society*, especially Chapter 5, 'The Woman Slave and Slave Resistance', pp.51-82; Herbert Aptheker, *American Negro Slave Revolts*, 5th edition, New York, International Publishers, 1987 (first edition, Columbia University Press, 1943); and Eugene D. Genovese, *From Rebellion to Revolution; Afro-American Slave Revolts in the Making of the New World*, New York, Vintage Books, 1981.

12. See Richard Price, *Maroon Societies; Rebel Slave Communities in the Americas*, 2nd edition, Baltimore, The Johns Hopkins University Press, 1979.

13. See Marietta Morrissey, *Slave Women in the New World: Gender Stratification in the Caribbean*, Lawrence, University Press of Kansas, 1989 for the thesis of women's reduced freedoms in the aftermath of slavery. See also Herbert Gutman, *The Black Family in Slavery and Freedom, 1750-1925*, New York, Vintage Press, 1976; Jacqueline Jones, *Labor of Love, Labor of Sorrow*; Leon Litwack, *Been in the Storm so Long: the Aftermath of Slavery*, New York, Vintage Press, 1980.

Liverpool and the English Slave Trade

DAVID RICHARDSON

English involvement in the African slave trade is generally thought to have begun in the mid-sixteenth century when John Hawkins made his celebrated voyages to West Africa and the Caribbean in the 1560s. But only with the 'Sugar Revolution' in Barbados in the 1640s and the resulting growth of demand for African labour in English America did the English become regular participants in the trade in African slaves. From 1660 to 1698 England's trade to Africa was dominated by London-based companies chartered by Charles II, the most important being the Royal African Company which held a monopoly of English trade to the continent from 1672 to 1698. The company's charter was challenged by 'interlopers' or private English traders, and was also strongly criticized by sugar planters who claimed that it failed to supply sufficient slaves to meet their needs. However, it is clear that by the end of the seventeenth century, largely as a result of the Royal African Company's activities, the English had become the

Fig.16
The Goree Warehouses, St George's Dock, Liverpool, by Samuel Austin, 1829
Named after the French island fortress off Senegal, the original warehouses were destroyed by fire in 1802 and rebuilt in 1811.

177
Oval épergne, by Pitts and Preedy, engraved with the arms of the Town of Liverpool and
those of Machell of Penny Bridge, Co. Lancaster, impaling Penny, with inscription. Presented
to James Penny in 1792 by the Liverpool Town Council in recognition
of his support for the slave trade.
Silver plate, 1792

88
Armed Brig in the Mersey
About 1810, by John Jenkinson (active 1790-1821), oil on canvas, signed

152
Punch pot
Hand painted with gilt decoration, earthenware, black ground, 1766

largest traffickers in slaves in the western world, shipping on average some six to eight thousand enslaved Africans a year to the Americas, over twice as many as the Dutch, their closest competitors.

The ending of the Royal African Company's monopoly in 1698 allowed private merchants legally to enter the slave trade. Thereafter, shipments of slaves in English vessels rose dramatically, averaging over 20,000 a year throughout most of the first half of the eighteenth century and reaching 30-45,000 a year during the rest of the century. The evidence suggests that, overall, almost 11,000 ships were fitted out in England for the slave trade between 1698 and 1807 and may have been responsible for transporting about three million Africans into slavery. This was equivalent to just under half of the estimated 6.7 million slaves shipped from Africa to America in the eighteenth century.

Merchants at London and Bristol dominated the English slave trade before 1730 and continued to be involved in it throughout the rest of the century. However, Liverpool ships began to enter the slave trade from the beginning of the century – the first known Liverpool slaver being the *Blessing*, which set out for Guinea in August 1700[1] – and by 1730 around 15 ships a year were leaving the port for the African coast. Thereafter, the number of ships fitted out in Liverpool for the slave trade climbed fairly steadily, growing to fifty or more a year in the 1750s and to just over one hundred a year in the early 1770s. Numbers of clearances from Liverpool to Africa then fell back during the War of American Independence in 1775-83. But they recovered strongly during the years after the war and reached 120-130 a year during the decade immediately preceding the abolition of the British slave trade in 1807.[2]

Of the 11,000 ships dispatched from England to Africa in the eighteenth century, approximately 5,300 (or 48 per cent) departed from Liverpool. Most of the remaining 5,700 slavers left from London and Bristol. These totals tend to underestimate the growing influence of Liverpool over the English slave trade as the eighteenth century progressed. Between 1780 and 1807 over three quarters of all English ships involved in the English slave trade were fitted out in the port. Thus Liverpool was not only the largest single English slaving port in the eighteenth century. After 1780, it was also the undisputed slaving capital of England and by far the largest slave port in the Atlantic world.

The reasons for Liverpool's rise to dominance of the English slave trade have long been debated. One argument offered is that, relatively marginalised in the transatlantic sugar and tobacco trades before 1750, Liverpool merchants proved more enterprising as slave traders than their rivals in London and Bristol. It is claimed, for instance, that they were more prepared than merchants at other ports to supply slaves illegally to the colonies of other nations, notably Spain and France.[3] Other writers have drawn attention to competitive advantages that Liverpool traders derived from the low level of wage rates in Lancashire before 1750, improvements in local port facilities, the relative freedom in wartime of Liverpool ships from attacks by enemy ships in British waters, and access to cotton textiles and other goods in demand in Africa. However, the relative importance of these factors is uncertain, and there still remains much room for debate about the causes of Liverpool's success as a slave port.

It is misleading to picture eighteenth-century Liverpool simply as a slave port. The city's merchants had close trading links with Ireland and western and southern Europe that preceded their involvement in the slave trade, and these continued to develop even as their interest in slaving grew. Furthermore, trade with other parts of the Atlantic world increased after 1700. Although Liverpool was never the principal English importer of sugar or tobacco, trade with the West Indies and the Chesapeake region in North America grew substantially in the eighteenth century. There was also a significant expansion of trade with the Newfoundland and Greenland fisheries and with the colonies of white settlement north of Maryland. For most eighteenth-century Liverpool merchants, therefore, slave-trading was only one of a number of commercial

78
Guinea
Gold, Royal African Company, 1663

82
Thomas Golightly
British School, oil on canvas, 19th century

pursuits followed.

Despite this proliferation of trading interests, it is clear that the traffic in enslaved Africans was the corner-stone of Liverpool overseas trade from about 1730 to 1807. This is reflected in the proportion of the port's shipping tonnage that was involved in the African trade. Thus during the 1730s about one sixth of Liverpool-owned shipping tonnage was involved each year in slaving voyages. This rose to over a quarter between 1750 and 1775. Thereafter, despite further increases in the tonnage of ships sent to Africa, the share of Liverpool shipping committed to slaving declined as trade with other areas, including the Americas, grew even faster. Even in the last years of the Liverpool slave trade, however, the African trade still employed about one sixth of the Liverpool fleet.[4] In addition, it appears that throughout the second half of the eighteenth century Liverpool merchants employed as much tonnage of shipping in trade with the West Indies as they did to Africa. Given the failure of newly imported African slaves to reproduce in the islands, the West Indies depended heavily on regular supplies of new African slaves to sustain their production of sugar and other exports. Moreover, some of the sugar and other goods carried from the islands by 'direct traders' comprised payments for African slaves delivered by other ships. In several ways, therefore, the slave trade was intimately linked with the growth of direct trade between Liverpool and the Caribbean. Taking this into account, it appears that the African and related trades may have occupied at least a third and possibly up to a half of Liverpool shipping tonnage in the half century before 1807.

Most of the ships sent from Liverpool to Africa were owned by Liverpudlians. We can only estimate the amount of capital that Liverpool merchants invested in the slave trade. It is clear that equipping ships for a slaving voyage to Africa was expensive, necessitating expenditures on the ship and its fittings, the hire of a crew of up to forty or fifty men, the provision of foodstuffs for the slaves in the Middle Passage, and the purchase of a cargo of trade goods to barter for slaves at the African coast.

Among the trade goods shipped were Indian fabrics, Manchester cottons, copper and brass wares, beads, liquor, firearms, and gunpowder. From merchants' accounts, it appears that the average cost of putting a slave ship to sea in the mid-eighteenth century was about £4,000, two thirds of which consisted of expenditures on trade goods.[5] As ships increased in size and the price of slaves in Africa rose, the cost of outfitting a slave ship mounted, reaching about £10-12,000 by the end of the century.[6] When combined with estimates of annual clearances to Africa, these figures suggest that about £200,000 a year was invested at Liverpool in the slave trade around 1750. This sum may have risen to over £1,000,000 a year by 1800.

The Liverpool slave trade attracted investment by individuals living in northern Lancashire and Cumbria, the West Riding of Yorkshire and the west Midlands. But most of the capital invested in the trade came from merchants, tradesman and shipmasters living in Liverpool and adjacent towns. To fund and organize voyages, these investors formed partnerships, the membership of which ranged in most cases from about three to eight individuals, though smaller or even larger partnerships can be discovered. Contemporary accounts suggest that the Liverpool slave trade attracted large numbers of small and occasional investors. But most of the funding and organization of the port's slaving activities revolved around a core of substantial and regular investors drawn mainly from the élite of eighteenth-century Liverpool commercial families such as the Blundells, Crosbies, Earles, Heywoods and Tarletons. As the trade in slaves was usually regarded as financially risky, the larger investors in the trade tended to spread their funds across several voyages simultaneously.

The contribution of the slave trade to the prosperity of eighteenth-century Liverpool cannot be measured precisely. Almost certainly, however, it was substantial. Historians continue to debate how profitable the slave trade was. Profits varied widely from voyage to voyage and some voyages were financial disasters, particularly where large numbers of slaves died in the notorious Atlantic crossing from Africa to America. Overall, returns on investments in the trade seem, nevertheless, to have averaged about eight to ten per cent a year in the second half of the eighteenth century.[7] Not surprisingly, investment in the African trade helped to bring substantial wealth to some of the principal Liverpool slave traders. For instance, John Tarleton, a major mid-eighteenth century African and West Indian merchant who became mayor of the city in 1764, saw his fortune climb from £6,000 in 1748 to nearly £80,000 in 1773.[8] Similarly, Thomas Leyland, who was a major slave merchant after 1783, co-founder of the bank of Leyland and Bullins, and several times mayor of Liverpool, was reputed to have been worth over £736,000 just before his death in 1827.[9]

While the slave trade helped to enrich some of the leading merchant families of Liverpool, it also brought employment and economic opportunities for many others in the city and surrounding towns. Some local merchants gained by supplying trade goods on commission to slave ships or by handling the sugar and other slave-produced goods imported in vessels returning from the Americas. Manufacturers in Warrington, St Helens and Manchester prospered through supplying the copper goods, glassware and cotton textiles that were exchanged for slaves at the African coast. Local tradesmen and seamen in Liverpool found work in building, fitting out, and manning the fifty to one hundred ships that regularly left Liverpool each year for Africa in the second half of the eighteenth century. Large proportions of those who sailed on slave ships failed, of course, to return to Liverpool, in many cases succumbing, like the Africans they were expected to supervise, to disease and ill treatment in the course of voyages. At the same time, some suppliers of goods

and other services to the slave fleet went bankrupt, victims perhaps of the financial uncertainties that surrounded the trade. Overall, however, the trade in enslaved Africans was a vital pillar of the eighteenth-century Liverpool economy, underpinning the substantial increase in the city's trade and shipping and promoting closer connections with the industrialising towns of Lancashire. Given such benefits, it is hardly surprising to find that Liverpool merchants were among the most vocal opponents of British abolition of the slave trade in 1807.

In retrospect, the fears of contemporaries about the impact of abolition upon Liverpool's fortunes proved to be misguided. Although prevented by law after 1807 from participating directly in the shipping of slaves, Liverpool merchants as well as Manchester manufacturers continued to supply English-produced trade goods to Spanish and Portuguese slave traders based in Cuba and Brazil throughout the early nineteenth century. In addition, Liverpool remained a significant importer of West Indian sugar and emerged after 1815 as the principal importer not only in England but in Europe of American raw cotton and West African palm oil. Both the latter were essential to the 'Industrial Revolution' that was occurring in north-west England at this time. Enslaved black labour was fundamental to the growth of both West Indian sugar until 1833 and raw cotton in the Southern United States until 1861. Moreover, it appears that much of the palm oil imported into Liverpool in the century after 1815 was produced by local slave labour within West Africa. Thus the shadow of slavery and the slave trade continued to hang over Liverpool's commercial history long after the city's status as the slaving capital of the Atlantic world had been ended by Parliamentary abolition of the English slave trade in 1807.

1. Liverpool Record Office, Norris Mss.

2. All figures relating to clearances are from D. Richardson, 'The Eighteenth-Century British Slave Trade: Estimates of its Volume and Coastal Distribution in Africa', *Research in Economic History*, xii, 1989, pp.185-95.

3. [James Wallace], *A General and Descriptive History of the Ancient and Present State of the Town of Liverpool*, Liverpool 1795.

4. For figures on clearances from Liverpool to Africa and all overseas destinations, see Liverpool Record Office, Holt and Gregson papers, 942 HOL X, 361-65, XIX, 69-71.

5. D. Richardson, 'Profits in the Liverpool Slave Trade: the Accounts of William Davenport, 1757-1784', in R. Anstey and P.E.H. Hair (eds.), *Liverpool, the African Slave Trade, and Abolition*, Liverpool, 1976.

6. R. Anstey, *The Atlantic Slave Trade and Abolition 1760-1810*, London 1975.

7. Richardson, 'Profits in the Liverpool Slave Trade'; Anstey, *Atlantic Slave Trade*.

8. Liverpool Record Office, Tarleton papers, 920 TAR 2/1.

9. L. Pressnell, *Country Banking in the Industrial Revolution*, Oxford 1956, p.419. Accounts relating to Leyland's slaving voyages are to be found in Liverpool Record Office, Leyland Papers, 387 MD 40-4; Harold Cohen Library, University of Liverpool, Ms. 10/46-52.

Oil not Slaves: Liverpool and West Africa after 1807

ANTHONY TIBBLES

'If our slave trade be gone, there's an end
to our lives:
Beggars all we must be, our children and
wives:
No ships from our port their proud sails
e'er would spread,
And our streets grown with grass, where
cows might be fed'
(Anonymous, Liverpool, c.1800)

The abolition of the slave trade by the British Parliament in 1807 might have been expected to have had a catastrophic effect on the economy of Liverpool. This was not the case, principally because Liverpool merchants continued to expand their bilateral trade with the Caribbean and the United States in those very goods – sugar, rum and increasingly tobacco and cotton – which had formed one arm of the triangular trade. Needless to say, these commodities were produced on plantations which were to rely on slave labour for many decades to come.

It is also true that Liverpool merchants continued to trade with West Africa, though on a more limited and less notorious basis. Initially attention focused on the goods which had brought Europeans to the West African coast before the large-scale involvement with slaving – gold, ivory and pepper. However, as early as 1800 small quantities of palm oil had been imported into Liverpool and it was this product which was to become the main trading interest for the next 100 years or more.[1]

Palm oil, extracted from the berries of palm trees, was recognised as a good lubricant and an important ingredient in soap. The introduction of metal machinery into industrial processes (for instance in the textile industry) brought with it a need for lubrication not found in smaller hand-operated machines. From the 1830s demand was spurred by the requirements of the railways. In the home, there was a rapidly growing demand for soap, particularly as industrial workers undertook dirtier jobs.

The pioneers of the trade came from Liverpool and were the same merchants who had been active in the slave trade – such men as John Tobin, James Penny, Jonas Bold and the Aspinall brothers. They used their experience and contacts in West Africa to develop this new trade. There was also a familiarity about it. The goods they were exporting were identical to those of the slave trade era – predominantly textiles, rum and guns. The Liverpool merchants quickly established a tight hold on the trade and sought to maintain a monopoly, which they were successful in doing for more than half a century.

The trade saw substantial growth and

substantial profit. A case in point is the career of John Tobin, who was Mayor of Liverpool in 1819 and was knighted two years later.[2] He was born in 1763 and had been involved in the slave trade first as a master and then as an owner. After 1807 he continued to trade to West Africa and was an early participant in the palm oil trade. In 1814 he imported 450 tons of oil. By 1832 this had risen to 4,000 tons. One of the main reasons for Tobin's success seems to have been his friendship and alliance with Duke Ephraim, an African chief at Calabar, who by the 1820s had a virtual monopoly of all trade in the area.[3] Others were similarly successful. By 1834 Tobin estimated that the trade in palm oil was worth half a million pounds.[4]

By this time the activities of the surviving slave traders, now dubbed 'illegal trade', were being seen as a frustration to what was referred to as the 'legitimate trade'. It was, therefore, for both economic and moral reasons that efforts were made to stamp out the slave traders and the British, who only a few decades before had been the major participants in the slave trade, became the major opponents. Anti-slavery patrols had been instigated in 1808 and in the 1820s, 1830s and 1840s up to a third of the Royal Navy was deployed off the West African coast. Not unnaturally some Africans found this confusing. Obi Ossai, king of Abo, put the matter very succinctly: "White people first told us we should sell slaves to them and we sold them; and White people are now telling us not to sell slaves. If White people give up buying, Black people will give up selling."[5]

By the early 1830s some of the new generation of merchants were becoming frustrated with the problems of the coastal trade and began considering direct trading links inland. They were encouraged by the explorations of the Lander brothers who had established the course of the Niger and shown that it provided a direct route into the interior. They not only recognised the commercial opportunities it offered but also saw it as a means of dealing a blow to the trade in slaves. The argument ran that only by encouraging proper trade, by encouraging Africans to produce raw materials that Europeans wanted

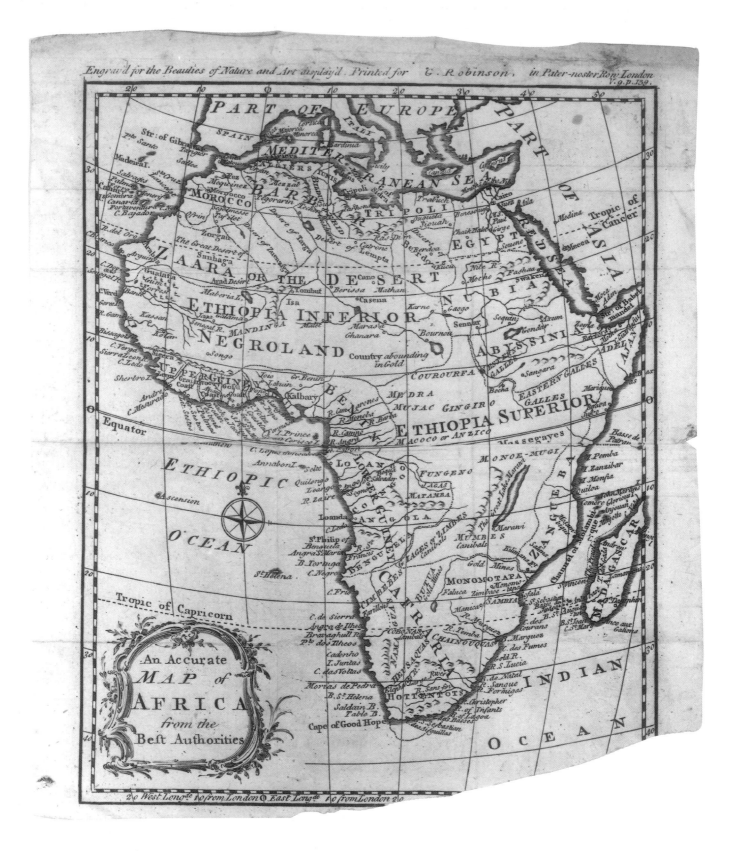

An Accurate MAP of AFRICA from the Best Authorities

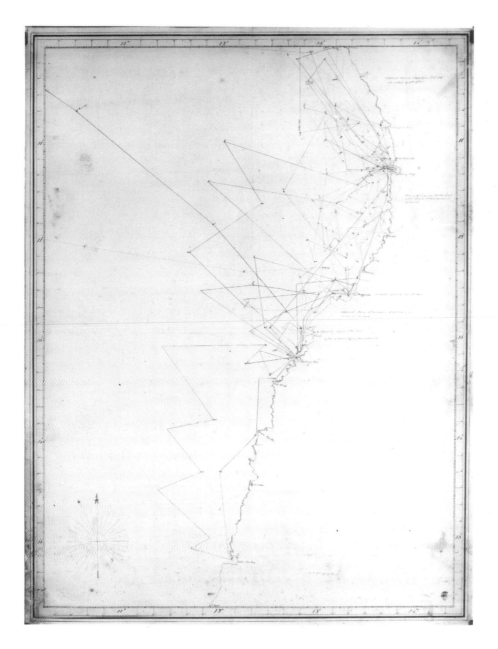

193
Manuscript Chart showing the tracks of a Royal Navy patrol vessel off the West African Coast
Facsimile of chart by Edward Smith, 1843

54 (opposite)
'An Accurate / MAP of / AFRICA / from the Best / Authorities'
London, 18th century

to buy, and by introducing Christianity, could the slave trade be eliminated. They were naturally opposed by the coastal traders and by the African middlemen who saw this as a threat to their livelihoods.

Again, the leaders of this movement were based in Liverpool and two of the main exponents were MacGregor Laird and Robert Jamieson. Both were Scottish by origin. Laird was born in Greenock in 1808 and was a son of William Laird, founder of the shipbuilding firm. His African activities are relatively well known. In particular, he instigated and led an expedition to the Niger in 1832,

building two steamships, the *Alburkah* and the *Quorra*, in Liverpool for the purpose. The expedition was a total failure: of 48 men only nine survived (highlighting one of the principal obstacles – the climate and problems of fever and disease). Laird lost a lot of money and, though continuing to support the cause, withdrew from active involvement for almost twenty years.

The standard was taken up by Robert Jamieson. Originally from Glasgow, he settled in Liverpool in the early 1830s (though from 1836 he also maintained a London home). He had extensive trading interests in South America, India and China, but was also involved in the palm oil trade. In 1839 he ordered a paddle steamer, which he named *Ethiope*, from the Liverpool shipbuilder, Thomas Wilson. The vessel left Liverpool in September 1839 and once in West Africa was placed under the command of John Beecroft, a man who had many years' experience as merchant and agent and was later to become British Consul at Fernando Po.

Beecroft's mission was to find a channel into the main body of the Niger, which avoided 'the pestiferous swamps of the Delta' and to 'establish a commercial intercourse with the interior'.[6] He was successful in finding a route through to the main river and in travelling to Rabba some four hundred miles from the coast.

However, the voyage also confirmed the difficulties of any inland trading enterprise: 'It remains then that commerce on the Niger can only be followed by means of steam-vessels manned entirely by native Africans, under the direction of European officers and engineers well inured to the climate. But even in this mode of prosecuting the desired intercourse, there appears too formidable an array of difficulties to render it likely to become of any considerable practical benefit to Africa or Europe – first, in the danger of navigating to and from Africa, vessels constructed so as to be of sufficiently light draught of water for the ascent of the rivers, and consequently badly adapted to the open sea – next, in the great expense attendant on the employment of steam-vessels in so distant a quarter and in such a cli-

194
'The celebrated piratical slaver L'Antonio with other of the black craft lying in the Bonny River'
Engraved by T. G. Dutton after N. M. Condy, 1845

mate – then in the impossibility of having them repaired in case of accident to the engineers, or of any serious injury to the machinery; and finally, in the fact, now well ascertained, that the river itself is not navigable except during the few months of the year when it is flooded.'[7]

Despite this frustrating conclusion, Jamieson instructed Beecroft to attempt an alternative route to the interior via the Old Calabar and Cross Rivers further east.

Meanwhile the efforts to establish trade with the interior were receiving support from another quarter, the British government of Lord Melbourne. It backed a so called Niger Expedition

which attempted to establish a European-style farm in the Lower Niger, and three Royal Navy steamers arrived in the river in 1841.

In fact, the expedition was opposed by many of those who might have been expected to welcome the initiative, including Jamieson and Laird. Jamieson was strongly against it and wrote three pamphlets on the subject starting with *An Appeal to the Government and People of Great Britain against the Proposed Niger Expedition* which he published in 1840. His case was economic – that free trade was superior to government intervention. He argued that once Europeans were given government money and became involved in agriculture, they

would want to protect their interest. They would want a chartered company, then a monopoly. It would force prices down, discourage African farmers who would cease to work towards a market economy and all development would end.

The Expedition was a total failure, but for a more immediate and obvious reason, namely fever. The settlers were decimated: 48 of the 145 were dead within two months and Jamieson's own *Ethiope* was called to assist in the rescue, escorting HM *Albert* down the Niger and back to Fernando Po.

Ethiope returned to Liverpool in 1843 but made further explorations of the Niger in 1845 and 1846. These voyages only confirmed Beecroft's initial assessment and although Jamieson continued to trade in palm oil he seems to have effectively given up exploration. However, the desire to establish direct trade inland did not die. In the mid-1850s MacGregor Laird returned to the scene and again undertook a series of expeditions into the interior using a number of new steam vessels which he built for the purpose. It was on one of these expeditions, under Dr Baikie, that the medical problem was eased when the efficacious effects of quinine were established. However, his attempts to set up trading stations were opposed by African middlemen and his ships were attacked on several occasions.

During his last years, Laird was preoccupied with these affairs, though writing in September 1858 he appears rather disillusioned: 'I suppose by next mail I shall hear something decided from the Niger, either that the *Sunbeam* is lost going up the river or has got up, or that she has put back under some pretence or other; if she is lost I am insured, if she has got up, I have no doubt she will make something of her cargo, if she has put back it will be a ruinous business – here again I have lost all confidence in the judgment of the man in charge of my property, I blame myself severely for going so headlong into such an outlay, as usual I see now what others could clearly see, whose passions and judgments were not warped by constantly thinking and dreaming of one idea, that the Agents you send out have quite a different standard to your own – they go to make money and that alone. I think they would make more by following their instructions but few can see more than immediate results.'[8]

Despite these setbacks Laird and Jamieson continued to believe in the desirability of establishing trade with the interior. In his *Commerce in Africa*, published in 1859, Jamieson urged the use of an alternative land route from the Cross River to the Niger as the way to avoid the swamps of the Delta.

It was, however, another of MacGregor Laird's initiatives which had the most profound effect on the way trade was to be conducted between Britain and West Africa in the future. In 1849 Laird founded the African Steamship Company and in 1852 contracted with the British Government to provide regular steamship services to carry the mails between England and West Africa.[9] This effectively gave him a subsidy for the new steam service. The introduction of steam liner services had a major impact on the palm oil trade and Liverpool's role in the region.

During the 1840s and 1850s, Liverpool's monopoly of trade in the region had been challenged by the entry of a number of small-scale merchants from Bristol and London eager to take advantage of the lucrative returns on palm oil. For a while, up to a third of the trade was taken by these new traders and Laird's initial decision to run the new steamer services from London seemed likely to reinforce this trend. However, in 1856 he re-located the steamers to Liverpool. Although the numbers of traders continued to increase, they used the new steam ships rather than their own vessels or tramp sailing ships and gravitated to Liverpool as the centre of their operations.[10]

Gradually the monopoly was re-established and by 1880 virtually all British palm oil imports were coming through Liverpool once more.

Ironically, at the West African end the opposite situation took place. Steamers could easily call at more ports and the effect was to diversify the sources of palm oil. The regularity and reliability of the services also drew other cargoes to the steamers so that Liverpool became the centre of virtually all West African trade.

The Liverpool-based shipping companies and their owners who ran the services worked closely together and saw off competition from other ports. By establishing agreed charges they protected their own positions. In later years this situation was consolidated by Sir Alfred Jones, who ran Elder Dempster, the main company, from 1884. Indeed, until recent years the name Elder Dempster was synonymous with the West African trade.

There was one further consequence of Liverpool's monopoly of the trade with West Africa. As Africans had been brought into Liverpool in the eighteenth century as a result of the slave trade, so these new trading links brought Africans into the port in the two centuries which followed. Elder Dempster employed Africans, particularly Kroomen, for much of the heavy work on board ship, though on poorer wages and conditions than their white counterparts. Many of these seamen found temporary residence in Liverpool and some established themselves permanently. In this way they contributed to the development of the black community in the city.

The links which the slave trade established between Liverpool and West Africa have endured for nearly three centuries. Despite the abolition of the trade in 1807, Liverpool's merchants found ways to exploit the experience which they had built up over the previous decades. Just as they had dominated the old 'African Trade', so they monopolized the new situation. The consequences of Liverpool's relationship with West Africa have been profound and far-reaching.

1. K. O. Dike, *Trade and Politics in the Niger Delta, 1830-1885*, Oxford 1956.

2. M. Lynn, 'Trade and Politics in 19th Century Liverpool: The Tobin and Horsfall families and Liverpool's African Trade', in *Transactions of the Historic Society for Lancashire and Cheshire*, cxlii, 1993, pp.99-120.

3. A. J. H. Latham, 'A Trading Alliance: Sir John Tobin and Duke Ephraim'in *History Today*, xxiv, 1974.

4. For a discussion on the profitability of the trade see M. Lynn, 'The Profitability of the Early Nineteenth Century Palm Oil Trade' in *African Economic History*, 1992, pp.77-97.

5. Dike, *op. cit.*, p.48.

6. 'On Benin and the Upper Course of the River Quorra or Niger', communicated by Robert Jamieson, *Journal of the Royal Geographical Society*, 1841, pp.184-193.

7. *Ibid*.

8. NMGM, Archives, DX.

9. P. N. Davies, *The Trade Makers*, London, 1973.

10. M. Lynn, 'From Sail to Steam: The Impact of the Steamship Services on the British Palm Oil Trade with West Africa, 1850-1890', *Journal of African History*, xxx, 1989, pp.227-45.

Fig.17
'Lowest Life in London', by George Cruickshank, 1823

Black People in Britain

JAMES WALVIN

Black people have lived in Britain for centuries. During the Roman occupation, for instance, a unit of African troops was stationed near Carlisle. There is evidence of Africans in York in the same period. Africans similarly found their way to many parts of Europe in the course of the Middle Ages. But from the late fifteenth century references to blacks begin to increase. There was a number of Africans at the court of King James IV of Scotland about 1500. Dunbar's poem *Ane Blak Moir* celebrated one such at the royal court.

By the last years of Elizabeth I, blacks were to be seen in London. Indeed, in 1596, the Queen sent a letter to the Lord Mayor of London complaining that: 'Her Majesty's understanding ... there are of late divers blackamoores brought into these realms, of which kind there are already here to manie [too many], considerynge how God had blessed this land with great increase of people'. The question arose again in a royal proclamation in 1601 which declared that the Queen 'is highly disconcerted to understand the great number of Negroes and blackamoores which (as she is informed) are carried into this realm since the troubles between her highness and the King of Spain ... [and] also for that the most of them are infidels having no understanding of Christ or his Gospel: hath given special commandment that the said kind of people shall be with all speed avoided and discharged out of this Her Majesty's realms'.

It seems that a number of these Africans were free people, possibly seized and freed from captured Portuguese and Spanish vessels. However, some Africans were brought directly to England. Early merchant adventurers had been instructed to import Africans and with the development of the early slave trade Africans began to acquire a price and a social cache. Time and again, British writers spoke of the exotic nature of black people living in Britain. The imported Africans were objects of fascination for people who had rarely seen black humanity before. Indeed, at royal masques and balls it was even common for people to dress up and blacken their faces.

However, once the British began to settle their colonies in the Americas, especially in the Caribbean from the 1620s onwards, they turned – like the Spaniards, Dutch and Portuguese before them – to Africa for labour. As the British ferried Africans across the Atlantic into Barbados, Virginia and Jamaica, it was inevitable that more and more of them would find their way – mainly as slaves – to Britain. They landed in British ports as slaves, or as personal servants to captains, sailors and returning settlers and military officials. In this way the foundations were laid for the early black communities in Britain.

The largest black community in the eighteenth century was to be found in London, understandably since this was the nation's largest port with the most numerous trading links to the slave colonies and Africa. As Liverpool's participation in the slave trade grew, so black people also appeared in that port. But blacks were to be found across the face of Britain, in most cities and even in the remotest of rural spots. The landed classes, retreating to their country seats, took their black servants with them. Time and again, commentators remarked on the black presence. In general, they were unskilled labouring people, most often employed as domestic servants. It is in that capacity that so many of them appear in contemporary paintings and pictures – part of the domestic scene in a stately home. But they were also used by artists to highlight the contrast between black and white

Some were slaves. They were imported as slaves, were bought and sold as slaves. We can tell that more and more were brought to England because of the increase during the eighteenth century in advertisements for the sale of slaves or the recapture of runaway slaves in English newspapers. Indeed, they provide us with rare glimpses of individual slaves:

A healthy Negro Girl aged about fifteen years; speaks English, works at her needle, washes well, does household work, and has had the small pox.
(*Daily Ledger* Dec.31 1761)

To be disposed of. A Negro Boy of 12 years old, extremely well made, good-natured, sensible and handy, speaks English well, and

has had the small Pox. Enquire at Mr Taylor's Barber's Shop, in Hart Lane, Covent Garden.
(*Daily Advertiser*, Feb. 11 1762)

Ran away from his Master, a Negro Boy, under 5 feet high, about 16 years old, named Charles, he is very ill made, being remarkably bow legged, hollow Backed and Potbellied; he had when he went away a coarse dark brown Linen Frock, a Thickset Waistcoat, very dirty Leather Breeches, and on his Head an Old Velvet jockey Cap.
(ca.1768)

Runaway, some Time since, a negro lad about 18 years of Age, near five Feet two inches high, answers to the name of Starling, and blows the French Horn very well.
(*British Journal*, 1757)

Ran away the first instant from Sir Phineas Pet at the Navy Office, a Negro about 16 years of age, pretty tall, he speaks English, but slow in speech, with a Livery of a dark coloured Cloth, lined with Blue, and so edged in the Seams, the Buttons Pewter, wearing a Cloth Cap, his Coat somewhat too short for him, he is called Othello.

There were, of course, a number of prominent, eye-catching black 'personalities' in Britain in the era of slavery. Billy Waters, 'King of the Beggars' (who lost a leg on a British warship), was buried with extraordinary popular pomp in 1823; Saartjie Baartman 'the Hottentot Venus' (a stripper who scandalised society); Bill Richmond and Tom Molineaux, the heavyweight boxers – these and others left their mark on the contemporary evidence.

But being a slave in Britain was different from being a slave in the slave colonies. First, it was unusual. In Jamaica, Barbados or Virginia slavery was the norm. In Britain it was wholly exceptional. In Britain, black slaves were surrounded by free people. Not surprisingly they often wanted to join them and to enjoy whatever benefits freedom had to offer. Some attempted to do so and, in London at least, a pocket of free blacks developed, keen to entice other slaves to join them – to run away and to leave their masters or mistresses for the uncertainties of freedom. Slave owners in England frequently complained of the free blacks who lured away their slaves.

English law was thrown into some confusion about their presence. Were they free in England – or were they slaves, like their contemporaries in the Americas? Throughout the eighteenth century English courts wavered, sometimes affording them the protection of the law, sometimes supporting their owners' claims that Africans were property – things – like slaves elsewhere. The property status of the black slaves in England was not finally resolved until slavery itself was abolished throughout British possessions in 1838.

The black community had its own favourite quarters and meeting places and its own distinct social life. In 1764 it was reported, for example, that 'no less than fifty-seven men and women, supped, drank, and entertained themselves with dancing and music, consisting of violins, French horns, and other instruments, at a public-house in Fleet Street, till four in the morning. No whites were allowed to be present, for all the performers were Blacks.'

When, in 1722, Lord Mansfield made his judgment that blacks could not be removed from England against their wishes, two hundred local blacks gathered: at 'a public house in Westminster to celebrate the triumph which their brother Somerset had obtained over Mr Stewart his master. Lord Mansfield's health was echoed round the room, and the evening was concluded with a ball. The tickets for admittance to this Black Assembly were 5s each.'

Most blacks in Britain were male and had domestic or poor labouring jobs, such as crossing sweepers. Some were beggars. After 1783, it was the poor blacks, especially those recently landed from North America, that caught the eye. To deal with these blacks, who had fought with the British against American independence, the government launched its ill fated Sierra Leone scheme to repatriate them to Africa in 1787. It was significant, perhaps, that the official – and charitable – response to the development of a poor black community was to seek ways of shipping it out, ostensibly back 'home'. Of course, for most of the blacks involved Sierra Leone was not, and never had been, home. It involved not merely a leap in the dark, but a dangerous return to the region of West Africa where slave trading continued to thrive.

Like other poor people living on the

161
Olaudah Equiano
British School, late 18th century

margins of society, poor blacks were often ensnared in the punitive legal system. We often catch glimpses of them from their acts of desperation, and from the consequent legal punishments, which from 1788 included transportation to Australia.

By the middle years of the eighteenth century, a number of commentators began to complain about the number of blacks living in Britain, though they tended to inflate the numbers involved, if only to prove their case. In 1764 it was reported in *The Gentleman's Magazine* that 'the practice of importing Negro servants into these kingdoms, is said to be already a grievance that requires a remedy, and yet it is everyday encouraged insomuch that the number in this metropolis only, is supposed to be near 20,000.'

Those who were most critical of the black presence were the West Indian planters and their friends. Yet it was often the planters, the slave traders and others who lived and worked in the slave colonies who brought slaves to Britain in the first place. This was a question which was more acutely debated after 1783, when the American slaves who had sided with the British in the recent War of American Independence came to Britain with their former masters.

What many of the West India lobby disliked was the fact that so many blacks were free. And even when, in principle, they were imported as slaves, many of them refused to accept their continuing bondage in Britain and simply ran away. They thus formed the basis for a black community which was prominent and readily visible in late eighteenth-century London.

But the black community had prominent friends – black and white – who, from the 1770s onwards, had raised the question of black freedom as a major social and political issue. The tide had begun to run against slavery, initially at least, within Britain itself.

From the 1780s a number of black spokesmen lent their voices to the cause of black freedom, denouncing slavery in general and specifically in Britain. The publications of Equiano and Cuguano, and their letters and contacts, added to the growing concern about the

163
The Black Boy
About 1844, by William Windus (1822–1907), oil on canvas

Fig.18
The Family of Sir William Young, ca.1766,
by Johann Zoffany, NMGM
(Walker Art Gallery)
Young, seated with a cello, came from a
plantation family in Antigua. He spent
most of his time in England despite
holding appointments in the West Indies.
His black servant is included in the group
of figures.

existence of slavery in Britain itself. Indeed, it now seems clear that the early
moves against slavery on a broader
front began with a criticism of slavery
in Britain.

Whatever the size of the black community, it evidently went into decline
in the years after the ending of the slave
trade in 1807. Thereafter, slaves were
too valuable in the West Indies to be
removed, for whatever reason, to Britain. Though other blacks settled in Britain in the early and mid-nineteenth
century, the black community in the era
of slavery was not to be matched in size
or importance until later in the nineteenth century, when new shipping
lines, especially to West Africa, helped
to create new black communities in British ports like Liverpool, London and
Cardiff.

1 Fuller accounts of the history of the black
people in Britain can be found in: P. Fryer,
*Staying Power: The History of the Black People
in Britain*, London 1984; F.O. Shyllon, *Black
Slaves in Britain*, Oxford 1974, and J. Walvin,
*Black and White: The Negro and English Soci-
ety, 1555-1945*, London 1973.

British Abolitionism, 1787-1838

JAMES WALVIN

173
Half-penny token, obverse: 'Am I Not A Man And A Brother', reverse: clasped hands, 'May Slavery & Oppression Cease Throughout The World'

At first sight, the British abolition movement was remarkably successful. Within twenty years of the movement's initial creation in 1787 the British Atlantic slave trade had been abolished. Later, when the movement had been reformed and revitalised after 1825, British slavery itself was abolished, between 1834 and 1838. No abolitionist in 1787 would have dared to hope that they would succeed so quickly and so thoroughly. But, of course, they were aided by forces they could scarcely understand, see or predict. What enabled the abolitionist movement to succeed were invisible forces transforming British life in conjunction with seismic changes among the slaves in the colonies. The abolitionist movement has, in large measure, been praised and rewarded for bringing the British slave system down. It is not to deny its importance – nor to minimise its crucial contribution – to claim that modern historians look for a much broader explanation for the end of the British slave system.

First, it is important to understand why abolitionists have received so much praise. The most prominent abolitionists (notably Thomas Clarkson and William Wilberforce) were great publicists, for themselves and their campaigns. Indeed it was part of their goal to establish in the British mind that they and their followers were the personification of the drive to end slavery. It was also an era which saw the unfolding of history in personal terms. This image, assiduously promoted by the powerful abolitionist propaganda machine, portrayed abolitionists as the good *versus* evil (slave owners). It provided an effective ploy. Moreover, after abolition in 1838, it was an image which was perpetuated by successive generations of nineteenth-century historians and commentators.

It is, of course, difficult to argue against that simplification without appearing to strip slavery of its gross immorality. And that, in a way, was a result of the work of the British abolitionists. What they did, quickly, unexpectedly and, in many respects, quite brilliantly, was to capture the high moral ground. Needless to say, the story was much more complex than that. Yet it

needs to be stressed that the triumph of abolitionism helped to establish the abolitionists' own interpretation as *the* explanation for the ending of British slavery. The mythology of abolition lived on to become part of the accepted canon of British historiography. In the years since 1945, however, new views have prevailed.

The origins of the British abolition movement were rooted in the influence of Enlightenment writing (most notably Montesquieu) and the development of British non-conformity. The majority of men in the first abolitionist group in 1787 were Quakers. Quaker groups had been created across the face of Britain from the early eighteenth century, and they gave the founding abolitionists an immediate national network. They were also – and crucially – a literate constituency. Moreover many of these activists were influential and prominent men whose authority and status were unimpeachable and who could, accordingly, secure respect and a hearing in their locality.

This embryonic network was galvanized, like much else, by the impact of 1789. The vocabulary of abolition was transformed by the vernacular of the French Revolution. Of course those very changes, which sent a surge of energy and inspiration through British abolition, also served to fortify the resistance and determination of the British established order. If abolitionists and radicals viewed 1789 as a reason to press on with their reforms, defenders of the British regime took 1789 as added reason to dig in.

Initially abolitionists were able to capitalise on the mood for reform by attracting remarkable numbers of signatures to abolitionist petitions which they submitted to Parliament. They issued cheap and plentiful tracts, simple publications which presented abolitionist arguments in a direct, crisp format to a British readership which was (at least in towns and cities) much more widespread than the government feared. We cannot tell how many people read this abolitionist literature. But we do know that it was consumed, in taverns, in coffee-houses, in private homes and in public meeting places, by the million.

The abolitionists' opponents – the

Fig.20
William Wilberforce, engraved by E. Finden
after G. Richmond.
Wilberforce (1759–1833) led the British
parliamentary campaign to abolish the slave
trade and slavery.

Fig.19 (opposite)
Thomas Clarkson with his treasure-chest of
samples of African produce and articles, painting
by A.E. Chalon
Clarkson (1760-1846) was a founder member of
the Society for Effecting the Abolition of the Slave
Trade in 1787.

West Indian planters, the Atlantic merchants and bankers and those with interests closely tied to the slave empire – were clearly taken by surprise. For more than a century they had thrived, unchallenged by questions of morality or economic utility, because they brought such amazing prosperity to Britain. Few could deny the wealth which flowed into the mother country. Whatever moral doubts may have existed, they remained the preserve of a minority. Moreover the incalculable suffering which the British slave empire had brought forth was far away in Africa, on the Atlantic crossings and in the slave colonies. There were, of course, thousands of Britons who knew what slavery really meant, most notably those men who worked on the slave ships and in the slave colonies, or those military and government officials who had spent part of their careers in the slave colonies. But they, too, stayed silent.

The slave lobby's case was simple and apparently irrefutable. The wealth which poured into Britain's major slave ports was massive and irreplaceable. Were the slave trade to end, it would bring the slave-based wealth of the Americas to a rapid conclusion. End the slave trade, they argued, and Britain would suffer massive economic loss.

For their part, the abolitionists adopted a different tack after 1787. Their basic premise was to attack the slave system of the Caribbean by ending the Atlantic slave trade. If Africans were no longer available to the planters – if they had to rely on existing slave populations for their labour force in the islands – the planters would be obliged to treat their slaves better. And if their treatment of slaves improved, the health of the population would improve, the population would flourish and, before long, a black peasantry would emerge which would provide the opportunity of free, rather than slave labour. It was, of course, a highly speculative venture. But it had the benefits of being specific and manageable.

From 1792, the abolitionists had lodged the issue of abolition inside Parliament. Thereafter it was subject to the whims and unpredictabilities of parliamentary moods and accidents. Indeed,

Patch box, with abolitionist motif, 'AM I
NOT A MAN AND A BROTHER'
Enamel on copper, South Staffordshire, c.1790

169 (opposite)
'African Hospitality', illustrating the
verse 'Dauntless they plunge amidst the
vengeful waves,/ And snatch from death
the lovely sinking fair'
Engraved by J R Smith, after George
Morland, 1 February 1791

167
William Roscoe (1753–1831)
After John Williamson (1751–1818), oil on
canvas

170 (opposite)
'Slave Trade', illustrating the verse
'Lo the poor captive with distraction
wild / Views his dear Partner torn from
his embrace!'
Engraved by J R Smith after George
Morland, 1 February 1791

mentary moods and accidents. Indeed,
had Wilberforce been a better manager
of votes, it is very likely that Parliament
would have passed abolition before
1807. There intervened, however, war
between Britain and France, the revolution in Haiti and a domestic attack on
British radicalism. From 1792 onwards,
a growing body of opinion, inside and
outside Parliament, feared demands for
change because they seemed to be influenced by France and because they
threatened to initiate the disasters
which the French experienced in St
Domingue. The slaves had begun to
play an obvious and undeniable role in
the debate about their own future. This
was to be the turning point in the story
of British abolition.

Initially, British MPs – and the prop-
ertied bodies which supported them –
recoiled from the idea even of discuss-
ing the end of the slave trade because it
seemed likely to threaten a reprise of
events in Haiti. It seemed, they claimed,
madness to debate abolition when in
the Caribbean there was a convulsion
among French slaves which threatened
to prove contagious. Indeed planters
throughout the region were deeply
alarmed about the spread of slave insurrection from one island to another.
The outcome was an effective end to
realistic prospects for ending the British slave trade for a decade. Ultimately
it took the ending of Pitt's regime and
the brief period of peace between Britain and France before abolition made
further headway. But when it did, in
1806, it rapidly passed through Parliament. By 1807 the British had ended
their Atlantic slave trade.

Thereafter – indeed for more than a
century – the British embarked on a new
crusade: to persuade other participants
in the trade to follow their own self-
righteous lead. Having turned their
backs on the slave trade, they sought to
make others follow their example. In-
voking morality and Christianity, but
using the power of the Royal Navy and
the diplomatic muscle of the Foreign
Office, the British set about imposing
abolition on the rest of the Atlantic
world. Needless to say few people were
impressed by this remarkable, almost
St Paul-like conversion. Other European nations viewed it differently. The

171
One Penny Token, obverse: chained slave
kneeling in supplication, 'Am I not a man
and a brother', reverse: Whatsoever / ye
would that / men should do / unto you,
do ye / even so to / them'
c. 1790

ish sincerity, the Iberians still had empires which demanded fresh Africans and the new U.S.A. was unhappy to follow the lead of its former colonial governor. But this varied opposition did not deter the British from pursuing what they regarded as their divinely appointed mission, to rid the Atlantic – indeed the wider world – of the scourge of the slave trade. Few of the British stood back to question the curiousness of their posture – slave poacher turned abolitionist game-keeper.

At the end of the European wars, the British used the Congress meetings to promote the case for international abolition, with varying degrees of success. They were also able to apply pressure through their ships and their diplomacy. Abolition in effect became a prominent aspect of British foreign policy for the rest of the nineteenth century. This international role caused intense irritation and grievance to other powers, most notably the French and Americans. The power of the British – buoyed up by expansive industrial wealth, reinforced by major international possessions, and implemented by a pre-eminent navy – masqueraded as a pious mission to safeguard virtue against the threats of evil. Opponents were more likely to see it in other terms.

British self-interest was no longer served by the slave trade. But if they sought to promote freedom, the new forms of economic prosperity that came with it suited, of course, a broad range of British interests. Freedom meant free trade, free labour, the free movement of capital, in effect the freedom of an ascendant British economy to invest, exploit and control – as best it could within the constraint of a new economic world system. Of course, this economic ideal had limitations. Nonetheless, it stood in marked contrast to the dominant ethos of the previous century. Freedom, not slavery, was the leitmotif of British Atlantic trade and business in the nineteenth century.

There was a brief respite, after the British abolition in 1807, before the abolitionists renewed their attack, on slavery itself. The gap was understandable. Firstly, the war consumed all energies and diverted all demands for change. But, perhaps more important, it was

essential to wait, to see what results were produced, in the islands, by the ending of the slave trade. By the early 1820s, when the first census returns from the slave islands had yielded their data (under the Registration Acts) it was clear that the slave population was in decline. This is exactly what planters had predicted. But it was merely a phase of a natural cycle, lasting only until young slaves, children when abolition was passed, entered their child-bearing years. From the mid-1820s the slave population began to pick up and grow, slowly but steadily. In the meantime, planters, faced with a possible decline in their slave labour force, began to reorganize their slave gangs. One result was that privileged slaves, and those who might have expected improvements, found themselves labouring in the fields. These reorganizations – necessary for the planters – served to increase discontent among the slaves.

There were other powerful forces for change among the slaves. First and foremost they were converting to Christianity, rapidly and universally in the British islands, notably to dissenting churches (Baptists and Methodists). With the end of the slave trade, more and more slaves were local-born as the Africans began to die out, and ever more of them were Christian. This had dramatic results which had long been feared by the planters but were generally unexpected by the missionaries. For a start it gave slaves an ideological unity which they had previously lacked. More than that, it gave them a direct bond with a growing band of abolitionists in Britain. Non-conformists in Britain were outraged to hear stories about the punishments inflicted on their black co-religionists. Thus, in an unusual twist, black and white came together as never before.

It was in the Caribbean islands that black Christianity produced its most fundamental changes. First, the new chapels provided slaves with a meeting place away from the plantations. Chapel also offered a forum for the emergence of powerful black preachers, steeped in the imagery and vocabulary of the Bible. The Old Testament, in particular, was replete with imagery with

direct relevance for people in bondage, awaiting salvation and freedom. Black Christianity deeply impressed visitors to the islands with its fervour, its noise, its enthusiasms. But its most impressive impact remained unnoticed at first, for it was crucially important in focusing the slaves' attention on their condition and raising their hopes of salvation to come.

Black church leaders demanded a salvation in the here and now. More and more slaves were unprepared to wait for the distant prospects of heavenly salvation. Its most potent expression took the form of major slave rebellions, in Barbados in 1816, in Demerara in 1823 and then, most seismic of all, in Jamaica in 1831-32. The causes were local of course. But running like a descant through it all was a rising sense of unease, in Britain, about the processes needed to keep slavery in place. The question was asked: if slavery could only be kept in place by violence on a truly medieval level, was slavery worth it? Here we touch on the other crucial element in the fluctuating story of British abolition. Britain itself was changing.

By the mid-1820s the British had lurched into the first phases of major urbanisation and industrial growth. A growing proportion of the people found themselves living in an urban habitat, where political organization was easier and where the printed word could circulate more freely and readily. Popular literature swirled through British towns as never before. For those who were interested, there were regular lectures on the abolitionist circuits. Tens of thousands turned up to listen to the abolitionist case. Indeed the only restraints on abolitionist lectures was the physical capacity of the meeting places. In all this women played an increasingly notable role. Thus, the printed and the spoken word swept up the British people in a well orchestrated movement.

From 1825 abolitionists turned to the petition as an expression of opinion. MPs were lobbied in their constituencies; they were in effect threatened that, unless they supported abolition in Parliament, abolitionists would direct their powerful armies of supporters against

trade and diplomacy

180
Plate with abolitionist motifs and mottoes
White china, printed in brown, early 19th century

182
Small cup with tropical scene and overseer
whipping a kneeling and chained slave
White china, printed in green, 19th century

181
Comport with abolitionist motifs and mottoes
White china, printed in brown, early 19th century

183
Sugar bowl
'East India sugar not made by slaves'
Stoneware, brown glazed, c.1822-34

184
Pair of figure groups, celebrating the end of slavery
Porcelain, painted in enamel colours, Staffordshire, c.1830-40

186
Medal, obverse: 'In commemoration of the extinction of colonial slavery throughout the British Dominions in the reign of William the IV Augt 1 1834', reverse: freed man standing in sunlight holding broken chains, 'This is the Lord's Doing: It is marvellous in our eyes Psalm 118 v.23 JUBILEE AUGT 1 1834'
J. Davis, 1834

the MP in any future election. Thus a groundswell of abolitionist sentiment was built up, in the country at large and within Parliament. The process was completed in 1832 by the Reform of Parliament. Though they inaugurated a system still far from democratic, the reforms swept away many of the old pro-slavery MPs, replacing them with men in favour of abolition. The abolition campaign had yielded good returns in its attention to constituency politics.

Thus, after 1832, it was only a matter of time before the British Parliament decided to end black slavery. It was disliked at home, disliked in Parliament and, of course, was hated by its victims throughout the slave islands. It was not merely coincidental that Britain ended slavery at the moment it found its broader economic interests switching. By the late eighteenth century, it was clear to many commentators (most notably Adam Smith) that the restraints on trade necessary to support the old slave empire were ultimately damaging. The argument took a different form among the small-time investors and speculators who – for all the fabulous wealth normally associated with slavery – were the typical backers of the slave system. Men and women with spare cash to invest found that profits were higher, and certainly less speculative, in house-building or in local business investments, than in ships and slaves. It was not so much that slavery became unprofitable, rather that other forms of economic activity were more attractive, less risky and more easily controlled.

Parliament brought slavery to end, partially, in 1834. It was terminated in 1838 throughout British colonies. Thereafter, abolition became a key factor in that cultural imperialism which became the hallmark of the British for a century and more.

The temptation of modern scholars is to see the abolition of the British slave system merely as a function of broadly based economic and social changes in Britain and the Caribbean. In part this is a healthy antidote to the older school which thought in terms of personalities and religion. Yet there has been a danger, in recent years, of undervaluing the abolitionist movement, and its prominent leaders. In truth they played a crucial role, for they acted as a catalyst, capitalising on those broader changes, often unconsciously. It was, after all, Parliament which abolished the slave trade and slavery. We need to know how and why that political change took place. The difficulty facing future historians is to explain the precise mix – the exact juncture – between the specifically political and the broad economic generalities. Though it seems doubtful that any future study will revert to an explanation focused on the abolitionists themselves, it would be wrong to marginalise them.

185
Medal, obverse: 'Jubilee in Commemoration of the Abolition of Slavery in the British Colonies in the reign of William IV Aug 1 1834', reverse: freed man, woman and child, raising arms to heaven 'Give Glory To God'
T. Halliday, 1834

187
Medal, obverse: William IV seated beneath canopy attended by 4 statesmen (Lords Grey, Rusell, Brougham and Althorp) 'I advocate the bill as a measure of humanity', reverse: Seven people hands joined dancing around a palm tree, 'Slavery abolished by Great Britain 1834'
Bronze, probably by T. Halliday, 1834

188
Plate with scene of former slave family in front of cabin, 'FREEDOM FIRST OF AUGUST 1838'
White earthenware with blue transfer-printing

The Impact of the Slave Trade on the Societies of West and Central Africa

PATRICK MANNING

29
Plaque showing Bini figures
Brass, Benin, 16/17th century

Africa is a vast continent with a large population made up of many cultures and societies. It was far more than a reservoir from which enslaved people were taken. The influence of the Atlantic slave trade brought turmoil and redirection to the lives of many Africans. It transformed their societies and lives, brought about population decline, built new kingdoms and destroyed old ones. It created systems for the gruesome work of collecting and exporting slaves, and brought the expansion of a system of slavery in Africa itself. The experience of the Atlantic slave trade tied West and West Central Africa tightly to the Atlantic world, and laid the groundwork for Africa's weakness and dependency in the world of today.

The basic story of the trade in enslaved people from West and Central Africa is well documented, and experts are in wide agreement on its outlines. But new research results continue to appear. Scholars approach the same evidence with differing outlooks – they come, for instance, from Europe, the Americas and Africa. As a result, scholars are engaged in important disputes over both fact and interpretation of the Atlantic slave trade. Most of the debates centre on the question, how seriously African society was harmed by the Atlantic slave trade.

Africa's contacts with the wider world were new but not unprecedented. Before the European voyages, African societies had contacts with each other and, through long-distance trade routes, with the Mediterranean world, western Asia and the Indian Ocean. New contacts came as Portuguese and then other European voyagers opened the West Coast of Africa to ties across the Atlantic.

The era of the Atlantic slave trade covered, at its maximum, over four hundred years from the mid-fifteenth century to the late nineteenth century. The changes in African life during the slave trade era are not a separate story or a sideline; they form one of the important elements in the story of the Atlantic slave trade as a whole.

In the first century or so of Atlantic contact, European visitors to Africa mostly sought gold and silver, and bought some spices. From the first, however, they also sought to capture and purchase slaves. European adventurers were always short of labour, and always seeking workers for agriculture and mining, and as servants and sailors. They sometimes captured and more often purchased captives along the African coast. This trade in chattel labourers gradually came to dominate all others.

The slave trade impacted Africa at the margins of its society in the fifteenth and sixteenth centuries, but the patterns set in those early days grew to importance in the seventeenth century. During the eighteenth and nineteenth centuries the exploitation of Africa for captive labourers hit its most severe peak. The effects of the Atlantic slave trade on African life are still visible as we come to the end of the twentieth century.

The availability of some African captives for purchase by early Europeans shows that slavery existed, in certain forms, in Africa before the Europeans. The fact of early African slavery has sometimes led to confusion, or to arguments that Africans, because they held slaves, were somehow responsible for the extent to which slavery expanded during the era of the Atlantic slave trade.

Rather than blame African victims or others, we should try to understand the operation of the whole Atlantic system and its reliance on enslaved labour. The new system – the Atlantic slave trade and modern African slavery – became quite different from early African slavery. In the early days, war captives and other dependents who fell under the control of African rulers did the bidding of their owners. Since medieval times, a sizable commerce across the Sahara had sent as many as 10,000 slaves in some years, mostly females, to serve masters in North Africa and the Middle East. But the number of persons held in slavery in Africa was small, since no economic or social system had developed for exploiting them.

After two or three centuries of the Atlantic slave trade, conditions in Africa had changed immensely. The five thousand slaves purchased by the Europeans each year in the sixteenth century had risen to nearly 100,000 per year

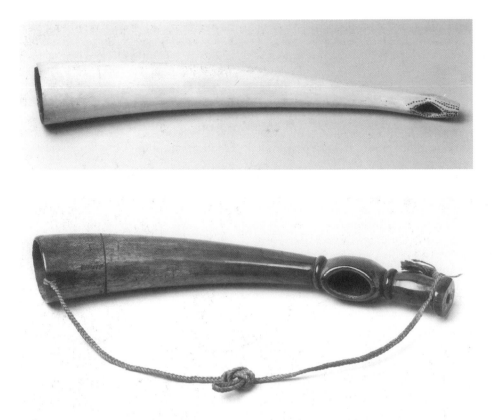

50
War trumpet
Ivory, Congo, 19th century

28
Trumpet
Mande, Gambia

at the end of the eighteenth century. By the end of the nineteenth century perhaps five or six million persons were held in slavery on the African continent, many times more than could have been enslaved before the Atlantic slave trade began.

The initial European purchases of slaves disrupted society in limited areas of Africa. Waves of this influence then spread wider and grew more forceful. In the sixteenth century, two types of patterns emerged, depending whether or not large states were involved in the slave trade. First, in Senegambia, Angola and the large kingdoms of Jolof and Kongo, the effects of the slave trade soon led to civil wars and disruption, which brought about the decline of the existing kingdoms on the one hand and the rise of new but smaller states on the other. One of the new states was the Portuguese colony of Angola, centred on the port of Luanda, from which Portuguese warriors and merchants exported several thousand slaves each year.

The second early pattern developed in Sierra Leone and nearby areas of the Upper Guinea Coast. In this region the slave trade proceeded more by kidnapping than by warfare. Some of the many captives were retained rather than exported, so that domestic enslavement, especially of women, expanded in the Upper Guinea Coast. While slavery expanded in the region, powerful states did not emerge.

In the seventeenth century, the sale of slaves grew so rapidly in the Bight of Benin that the region became known as the Slave Coast. Later in the same century some adventurers in the neighbouring Gold Coast found the rising prices of slaves so attractive that they gave up their interests in gold mining and trading in goods, and turned to the capture and export of slaves. In both of these areas, the wars accompanying the development of large-scale slave exports led to the creation of powerful states: Dahomey in the Bight of Benin and Asante on the Gold Coast.

The social transformations of these areas involved far more than the creation of powerful monarchies. The population of both regions, and especially of the Bight of Benin, declined for

Fig.21
Danish traders negotiating with the
Akwamu king in 1784, from P. E. Isert,
*Neue Reise nach Guinea und den Caraibischen
Inseln*, Copenhagen, 1788. The Danes
sought the support of the Akwamu to
defeat the Awuma people who were
opposing completion of a Danish fort, seen
in the background.

decades as a result of the continued
warfare and export of slaves. In addition, since most of the captives sent
across the Atlantic were male, these
areas of the West African coast and its
hinterland were left with a shortage of
men. Many of the women who remained were now in slavery because of
the wars. Women had to take on new
tasks to sustain the economy, and the
remaining men found it easier to take
on second and third wives.

Slave exports from the Bight of Benin
and the Gold Coast reached a peak
about the 1720s, and declined somewhat thereafter – in part because the regional populations were now declining.
Slave merchants then found new regions of the coast to draw into slave
exports.

From the 1720s to the 1750s two
forested regions without large kingdoms became the main new sources of

slaves. These were the equatorial forest of the Congo (or Zaire) river basin,
and the Bight of Biafra, populated especially by Ibo-speaking peoples. In
both of these areas the demand for
slaves and the rewards of selling them
caused the development of new systems of delivering slaves. Slaves were
captured primarily by individual kidnapping and by the sentencing of
people to enslavement by court systems, following the earlier pattern of
Upper Guinea. Through these devices,
large numbers of people were taken to
the coast and sold to European merchants, without, however, the formation
of large kingdoms and massive raids of
other parts of the continent. Perhaps
the number of casualties was propor-
tionately smaller in these areas. Nevertheless the export of people, besides
the deaths due to exposure on long trips
to the coast, was sufficient to cause the

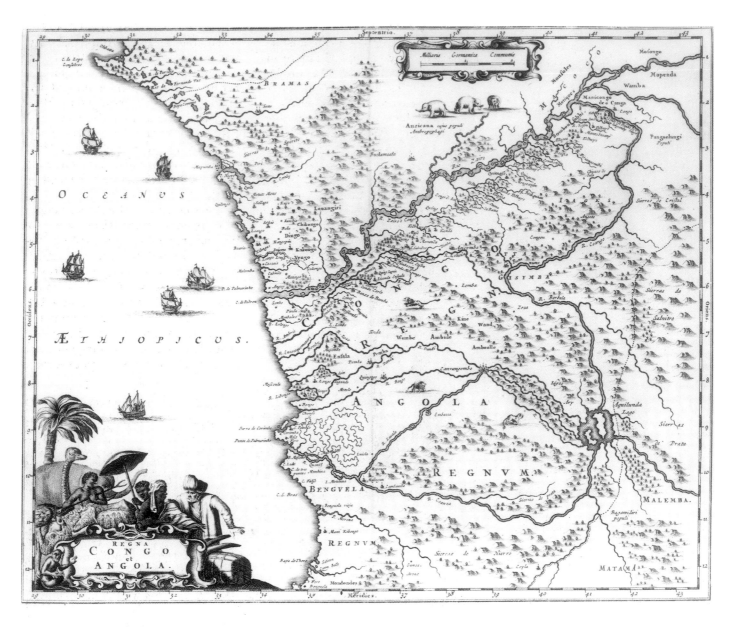

52
Map of Congo and Angola
John Ogilby, London 1670

populations of each of these areas to decline for much of the eighteenth century and some of the nineteenth century.

In the Bight of Benin in the nineteenth century the rise of one great kingdom and the fall of another brought decades of warfare. The Sokoto Caliphate, a Muslim empire, rose just after 1800 to control all of what is today northern Nigeria and adjoining areas, and the neighbouring Oyo empire collapsed three decades later. These wars brought enslavement for hundreds of thousands, and deportation – to the Atlantic or the Sahara – for many of them.

Finally Angola, already one of the centres of slave exports two centuries earlier, was drawn after 1810 into exports on the greatest scale in the history of the Atlantic slave trade. Three state systems combined to collect captives and relay them to the coast: Portuguese-ruled Angola on the coast, Kazembe in the inland valleys and Lunda in the savannas of the far interior.

These are some of the stories of the exports of slaves from Africa. But equally important are the stories of the changes in life for those who managed to remain in Africa.

After years of research and debate, scholars are now fairly well agreed on the number of people who underwent the Middle Passage: Paul Lovejoy's estimate of some twelve million persons loaded on ships at the African coastline is one most would accept. Far more difficult to agree, however, is the number of other Africans directly affected by the trade. This includes not only those who died on shipboard, but those who died during capture or during transportation within Africa, and the large number of enslaved people who remained in Africa or were traded to the Indian Ocean, Asia and North Africa. All agree that such a total is well beyond twelve million; research in progress may help reveal the details.

Where the slaves came from is also known in increasing detail. The regions of coast through which the greatest number of people passed were Angola, the Bight of Benin, Congo, and the Bight of Biafra, though other areas also lost large numbers of people. Debates continue on the ethnic origin of captives from each area of the continent, and on whether most captives came from near the coast or from the far interior. Recent research is showing that children became an increasingly important part of the Atlantic slave trade. One pattern is clear: while male slaves came from both the coast and the interior, female slaves came overwhelmingly from coastal areas. Women enslaved in the interior of Africa tended to be kept by African owners.

The overall size of the African population remains under debate. Views on the topic range from asserting that the slave trade had no effect on African population to estimating a drastic population decline. The most detailed recent research indicates a slow but steady decline in African population during the eighteenth and nineteenth centuries, an overall shortage of men, and local effects that were quite serious.

53
Map of Africa, printed and coloured
Probably from Ortelius, *Theatrum Orbis Terrarum*, Antwerp, 1570

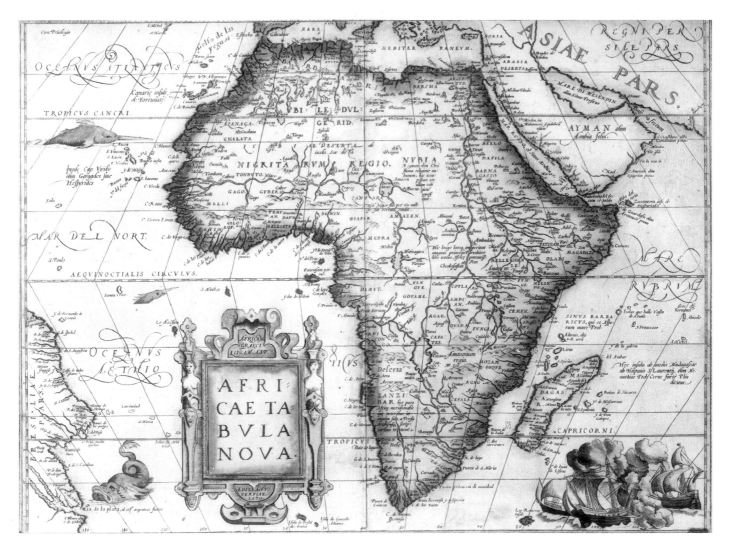

The demographic losses due to slave trading consisted not simply in the numbers of persons sent overseas, but deaths in the course of capture and transport within Africa, and the loss of reproductive potential as young women were sent away.

The growth of slavery within Africa during the era of slave exports has become a major focus of research and debate. The dominant view is that slavery in Africa expanded through ties to the export slave trade, and remained important after the export trade declined. Slaves became most numerous in the parts of Africa where there were strong states, such as the Sokoto Caliphate, to keep them in submission, but slavery expanded to a lesser degree in such areas as the Congo basin and the Bight of Biafra where states were small. In Africa as in the Americas, some slaves escaped and formed maroon settlements. European conquest of Africa, in the years surrounding 1900, halted raiding for new captives but did not liberate those already enslaved. As late as the 1920s, millions of people in Africa had still not gained their freedom.

The impact of the slave trade on African political life has been complex and contradictory. From the earliest campaigns for abolition, a debate has raged on the question whether the slave trade stimulated war in Africa. Those who say 'no' point to the stated war aims of participants in African wars, and note that the parties had other grievances and more specific objectives. Those who say 'yes' note the overall correlation between demand for slaves and the frequency of warfare. A parallel and unresolved debate continues between those who point out that the slave trade caused people to join in larger political units for protection, and those who emphasize that enslavement and greed caused the break-up of numerous states.

Similarly, the slave trade both created and destroyed fortunes in Africa. New social classes – of merchants, warlords and slaves – emerged in many areas of the continent. The export of slaves brought wealth to the African sellers, but very little of this wealth could be invested in expanding African production. Without slave exports, Africa would have had fewer imported goods, but would also have lost fewer productive labourers. As it was, many slaves were exchanged for various forms of money, and one ironic result of the Atlantic slave trade is that it expanded the money economy in Africa. The result did not make the continent any richer: the consensus among scholars is that the slave trade was bad for African economies. The remaining questions are by how much, and how African societies were induced to participate in the downward spiral of slave trade. Research in progress on the prices of slaves in Africa and around the Atlantic will clarify these issues. It will also help answer the question of how much effect the British anti-slavery squadron had in suppressing the slave trade after 1808.

The long experience of the slave trade must have had a profound effect on the thinking of Africans. These patterns of thought are not yet well documented, but we can hint at them. Slavery and the slave trade seem to have brought contradictory experiences and contradictory ideas. On one hand it brought dreams of wealth and power, as seen in the great commercial city of Kano, the golden regalia of Asante, or the imposing royal statuary of Dahomey. On the other hand it brought the rejection of hierarchy and a strong desire for independence and equality. This egalitarian ideal is evident in the willingness of people to live in isolated villages to avoid submitting to slave raiders, and in the development of an artistic tradition, abstract in form, that emphasized ties to the ancestors and to such basic life forces as the earth. The position of women in African society today reflects both sides of this earlier choice: women play full and independent social roles, especially in commerce; yet the majority of slaves in Africa were women, and all women have suffered some oppression as a result. The widespread significance of divination (to learn the future) and common fears of witchcraft in Africa owe something to the uncertainty of life brought by centuries of slave trading. In these and other ways, the Atlantic slave trade changed the thinking of Africans.

Europeans conquered Africa in the years surrounding 1900. As the new

46
Plaque showing European with gun
Brass, Benin, 16/17th century

47
Trade gun, known as a dane gun

48
Weights representing a) a man with gun, b) a gun, c) a cannon
Brass, Asante, Ghana, c.18th century

94
Flintlock blunderbuss
English, late 18th century

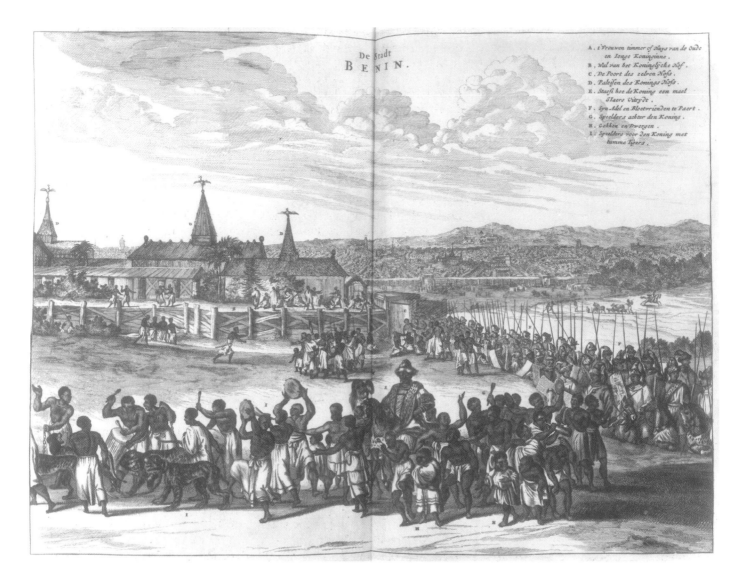

A . 't Vrouwen timmer of huys van de Oude en Ionge Koninginne .
B . Wal van het Koninglijcke Hof .
C . De Poort des zelven Hofs .
D . Paleisen des Konings Hofs .
E . Staesi hoe de Koning een mael Staers Uytrydt .
F . Syn Adel en Bloetvrienden te Paert .
G . Speelders achter den Koning .
H . Gebben en Dwergen .
I . Speelders voor den Koning met kumme Speers .

Fig.22
A procession of the Oba in the City of Benin, from Olfert Dapper, *Nauwkeurige Beschrijvinge der Afrikaansche Gewesten*, Amsterdam, 1668
The Oba or king is shown processing with a group of musicians and warriors with a view of the city of Benin in the background.

39
Kuduo, cylindrical base on cage-shaped stand
Brass, Asante, Ghana, c.1730-49

rulers established direct control over African societies, and began to learn in detail about Africa, they often portrayed themselves as bringing about the first contact of Africans with the outside world. The reality was quite the contrary. Even though few Europeans had visited the African interior, West and Central Africa had been in close contact with the Atlantic world for four hundred years already, and those contacts had grown more intensive with each succeeding century. Unfortunately, the contact was dominated by the Atlantic slave trade, with its corrosive effects for the peoples of the African continent.

An African View of Transatlantic Slavery and the Role of Oral Testimony in Creating a New Legacy

MARY E. MODUPE
KOLAWOLE

To the African, slavery in any form is considered to be one of the most dehumanising and degrading aspects of human experience. The fact that African domestic slavery pre-dates transatlantic slavery does not change this position. Slavery is regarded in the African world-view as an undue intimidation and oppression of everyman by the royal class, or of the poor by the rich. Africans view the imposition of transatlantic slavery as an act that cannot be vindicated simply because slavery had existed, in one form or another, since before the time of the Roman empire. Jo Freeman highlights the long standing existence of slavery in ancient European civilisation and in particular, women's space in those societies: 'Roman law was an improvement over the Greek society. In that cradle of democracy only men could be citizens in the polis. In fact most women were slaves and most slaves were women ... In ancient Rome ... women and slaves could not assume proprietorship and in fact frequently were considered to be forms of property'.[1]

The nature of human interaction between African and European was inevitably conditioned by this existing social structure during the 'Age of Discoveries' of the fifteenth and sixteenth centuries when European exploration, maritime expertise and commercial activities increased in scope. Transatlantic slavery as an historical transaction has its origins in Portuguese exploration of the West Coast of Africa and their establishment of trading stations such as El Mina on the Gold Coast (Ghana). The Spanish and the Portuguese found the new West African routes useful alternatives to the East, enabling them to obtain spices directly, without the Arab middlemen. Africans then became involuntary participants. Some important decisions that were to affect Africa's very existence were taken without consulting the Africans. In 1494, the Treaty of Tordesillas, a precursor of the Berlin conference of 1884, shared out the world between Spain and Portugal, allocating Africa to Portugal.

Other Europeans – the French, the Dutch, the British and, to some extent, the Germans – followed suit. The tripartite trade became focused on African slaves as the most profitable commodity and source of wealth for the European plantation owners in the West Indies. Since Europeans and Indian indentured servants found the harsh, hot, tropical conditions unbearable, Africans who were used to such natural conditions became valuable assets to the plantation owners. They were generally treated as commodities with no human or legal rights. The enormity of the scope of transatlantic slavery and the level of human agony, as well as its impact and implication on the history of three continents, make it unique.

The plantation owners were not insensitive to the moral implication of the racially constructed transatlantic slave trade, and its obvious contradiction of Christian teachings and ideals. They were therefore quick in adducing various reasons and finding justification for their inhuman activity. Some Europeans argued that slavery already existed in Africa and that the transatlantic form provided better conditions and a chance to 'civilise' Africans. Some writers still try to validate transatlantic slavery to alleviate the sense of guilt. Many western writers nonetheless document it with scholarly sincerity and integrity. It is, however, generally accepted that African slaves formed the backbone of European economic enrichment in the Caribbean colonies and contributed directly and indirectly to European economic and industrial growth.

African labour became indispensable and this accounts for the duration and continuous attraction to slavery. Inevitably, the transatlantic slave trade created an African diaspora in Europe and the Americas. The consequences, in the creation of a new legacy and new racist ideologies, are ubiquitous, shaping several aspects of the lives of Africans, Europeans and Americans today. Many people believe that the wealth of cities such as Liverpool is inextricably linked to the transatlantic slave trade. In Africa, imperialism, colonialism and neocolonialism became permanently entrenched in the mind, thought and experience of the people. The far-reaching consequences of these new alien concepts, ideologies and political structures determined the subsequent growth or diminishing of existing Afri-

Fig.23
A coffle
Captives were marched, often in yokes, from the inland areas of Africa to the coast for sale to Europeans.

can civilisations, art, culture, architecture, education and technology.

Africans, however, attempt to revisit history through anthropological, archaeological, oral literary, oral historical and diverse other sources to objectify the experience and portray the transatlantic slave trade from the horse's mouth. To the African, the devastation suffered physically, psychologically, emotionally and morally almost defies atonement. Indeed, some of the socio-political problems that are peculiar to blacks in the Diaspora today take root in a scene of an omni-present past and historical injustice. Although domestic slavery in Africa predates the transatlantic slave trade, it is essential to reiterate that there is a wide gap between the motive, nature, practice and implication of the two forms of enslavement. Domestic slavery was not racially constructed, nor did it involve the repugnant scope of degradation, geographical dislocation, cultural disorientation or forced acclimatisation and

attendant devastation and death.

African domestic slavery was characterized mostly by the rich, as well as powerful kings and chiefs, enslaving others. Slaves, therefore, included war captives, the kidnapped, adulterers and other criminals and outcasts. Every form of enslavement carries within it the germ of cruelty and degradation. But domestic slavery in Africa did not embrace the excessive dehumanisation involved in the new form of enslavement. Palace chiefs in many parts of Africa, though slaves, enjoyed certain privileges that were envied by lower-class and poor free people. Royal slaves of the Alafin of Oyo and Ooni of Ife were highly regarded because they had privileged access to the king and could even seek favours from him. They sometimes enjoyed relative affluence and a prestigious position, like those of Ilari slaves (slave officials). Odi slaves in Ijebu palaces were known to have a special status as well.

49
Yoke
West Africa, 19th century

African women's peculiar degradation in transatlantic slavery

In traditional African slavery, women slaves were often domestic hands to the rich and they enjoyed a better condition of life than some free women. Women leaders such as Madam Tinubu of Abeokuta and Lagos as well as Queen Amina of Zaria had many female slaves. Although malestream documents present them as cruel rulers, a female Ooni of Ife, Olowu, used slaves productively for making terraced roads invented by using local pottery pieces. These can still be seen in some parts of Ile-Ife today.[2] Another form of domestic slavery was the Iwofa or *iwefa*, a means of holding people as a ransom until a debt was redeemed. This was a transient and conditional form of enslavement. In many parts of West Africa, slaves could redeem themselves and earn their freedom.

The transatlantic slavery, however, brought an indescribable level of agony and unprecedented quest for enslavement because of the increasing desire for European goods such as alcohol, tobacco, firearms and other items. Forced and more permanent separation and harrowing, tumultuous experience followed, as people, usually youthful, robust men and women at the most productive age, were extracted and uprooted from their family, friends and fatherland. In all this, women as mothers felt the agony more profoundly. The lure of better conditions in Europe and the Americas was not justified by attendant emotional, physical and psychological trauma and dehumanisation. Women often had their children kidnapped and enslaved in their absence while slave women were often separated forcibly from their enslaved children.

The transatlantic slave trade brought new levels of degradation and suffering to women because the intensified attraction of European goods made Africans more greedy to acquire slaves. The availability of European firearms intensified inter-tribal and intra-tribal wars, especially as more prisoners of war meant more slaves and more firearms. Africans became hardened and women received the butt-end of this callousness. Men married more wives to produce more children, a ready source for the slave market! Some African slave owners were more eager to sell female slaves off to Europeans as they kept male slaves for agricultural and professional roles such as palace drummers. Between 1724 and 1727, King Agaja of Dahomey sold large numbers of female slaves before the loss of Ouidah (Whydah) curtailed his trade.[3] An understanding of African women's exaltation of motherhood and mothering will depict the intensity of the African woman's agony during this nadir of human degradation. Women's dignity and self-esteem were violated during slavery and the subsequent Middle Passage and it continued till the post-bellum period in the Diaspora.

African women's resistance and resilience

The erroneous impression is often created that African women took enslavement, like subjugation and subordination, for granted as a normal fact of their reality and so did not resist transatlantic slavery. On the contrary, documents show us that they resisted European subjugation just like men. Slave revolts, insurrections in Africa, *en route* and on the plantations in the Diaspora did not exclude women. Women were involved directly or indirectly in resistance against King Afonso I in the Congo (1529), Guinea slave traders (1556), in Sao Tome (1560) and the Macingo rebellion (1570).

African warfare between the sixteenth and the nineteenth centuries depended largely on metaphysical and psychological aspects and women were indispensable in these. Yet African women's roles were not adequately documented until recent research on women's resistance in the pre-colonial, colonial and post-colonial periods.[4]

Many European explorers, historians and colonial administrators have given subjective and inaccurate accounts of women's docility and lack of resistance. Thomas Winterbottom wrote: 'In Africa, women are regarded as beings of an inferior nature, and as born to be the

17
Robe
Woven indigo-dyed cotton embroidered with white cotton, Hausa, Nigeria

16
Comb
Carved wood, Old Calabar,
Nigeria

The role of oral literature and history and the creation of a legacy

Oral literature and history play an important role in highlighting the nature of the experience of slavery, of resistance and the creation of a new legacy in the African Diaspora. Some measure of cultural continuity was achieved through oral tradition and language. Women played a vital role in their preservation and they deployed oral poetry, folk-tales and anecdotes to create an African cultural base that is, for example, the prototype of the Brer Rabbit and Uncle Remus tales. Cultural transmission was an effective tool of resilience and resistance as slaves refused to allow the trauma to destroy their identities completely.

Women used oral as well as written poems, songs, folk-tales, proverbs, anecdotes, parables and fables to transpose African culture to the new world as well as relive their African experience. This oral genre pre-dated the slave narratives by Olaudah Equiano and others. It was also antecedent to works by modern writers such as Zora Neale Hurston, Ralph Ellison, Edgar Wright, Maryse Conde, Alice Walker and others.

There are many aspects of transatlantic slavery that have remained controversial. Generally, Africans focus on the indescribable, even irreparable, damage and trauma caused by this peculiar human interaction. Eurocentric scholars attempt to vindicate or provide an apologia, while theorizing about the normalcy of slavery and its indigenous nature in Africa. Africans in the Diaspora continue to seek a meeting point between their African heritage and the inevitable reality that they have come to stay in the Diaspora and have acquired new sets of values which must necessarily be properly integrated. This paradox of cultural identity in a multicultural setting continues to inform the search for new directions. Cultural enrichment through literature, music, dance, the arts, fashion and cookery, among other activities, are aspects of European and American realities today.

Women of African origin in the

slaves of men ...'.[5] Ironically, he portrays the Mandingo slave revolt in Sierra Leone (1785-86) which was not an all-male uprising.

African female forms of resistance included poisoning slave owners or contaminating their food. Others adopted mystic curses that were believed to be potent and at least frightened some slave owners if invoked by an angry slave. Others even tried to escape or commit suicide as an alternative to degradation and dehumanisation. Revolts in slave warehouses at El Mina castle, Goree, Luanda, Zanziba and Mombasa cut across gender lines. The acme of slave women's revolt, resistance and resilience is seen in the role of the Amazon warriors in Dahomey, who consisted largely of female slaves. They were crucial to the attacks and plundering of European slave forts and factories. Women also constituted a formidable force in attacks on baracoons.

In Dahomey, under King Agaja, women slaves dominated the army and they were crucial in the protective role of frontier guards. They resisted local incursions from neighbours like the Egbas as well as European slave traders. King Behazin's one thousand wives were central to the resistance against Germans, although he was later captured. The Amazon warriors, consisting largely of women slaves, were always troublesome to captors. Eight thousand Amazons resisted Beecroft in 1851.[6] According to Hosen Joffe, organized resistance in various parts of Africa retarded slavery: 'Resistance saved whole villages untold millions of lives, engineered many escapes, frightened off many slaving expeditions ...'.[7] Women acted as motivators where they were not activators. They also took part in predatory expeditions and slave conspiracies and insurrections.

25
Calabash guitar with bow
West Africa

22
Bow lyre
Leather, wood and string, West Africa

26
Small drum with drum stick
West Africa

132
Drum
Wood, cedar root and deer skin, Virginia, late 17th century

134
Marimbola, with red, black and white painting
Wood, Loiza Aldea, Puerto Rico, 1950

Americas and the Caribbean play a leading role in the search for meaningful relocation and empowerment in the new multi-cultural setting of the Diaspora. There has been an increase in the quest for a new identity in a move to explore the past, especially the transatlantic slave trade, to explicate the present and carve new positive paths for the future. These women tell their stories without self-pity while exploring African arts, literature, folklore, philosophy, fashion, religion, even cookery, to recreate their African heritage and experience. The new quest for cultural discovery and recovery in the last half of the twentieth century is a direct result of the role of women in transmitting African values through story-telling, poetry, song and dance, inter alia.[8]

In her research into African legacy in the Caribbean, Maureen Warner-Lewis (she adopted the Yoruba name Morenike) identifies the centrality of music, oral poetry, literature and oral history in 'stimulating and sustaining memory'.[9] She recorded about one hundred and fifty songs in the Yoruba language that are still actively sung by Trinidad elders. Many of her informant-singers are women. These relics from the past emphasize the survival of African culture largely due to women's resilience. Much Trinidadian oral poetry still reveals Yoruba metaphor, form and world-view today.[10] The minor-key calypso is believed to have considerable Yoruba influence as well, and this is true of other literary and artistic forms by Africans in the Diaspora.[11] One can conclude that apart from positive legacies, some contemporary problems such as racism are legacies of the transatlantic slave trade that the world continues to confront.

1. Jo Freeman, 'The Building of the Gilded Cage' in Ann Koedt et al., Racial Feminism, New York, Quadrangle, 1973, p.129.

2. David Sweetman, Women Leaders in African History, Oxford, Heinemann, 1984.

3. I. A. Akinjogbin, Dahomey and Its Neighbours, 1708-1818, Cambridge, Cambridge University Press, 1967.

4. Nina Emma Mba, Nigerian Women Mobilised, Berkeley, University of California, 1982.

5. Thomas Winterbottom, An Account of the Native Africans, vol. 1, London, Frank Cass, 1969, ch. IX, pp.144-54.

6. Saburi Biobaku, The Egbas and Their Neighbours, Oxford, Clarendon Press, 1965, pp.34ff.

7. Hosen Joffe, A History of Africa, New Jersey 1885, p.48.

8. bell hooks, Yearning, Race, Gender and Cultural Politics, Boston MA, Southend Press, 1990; Leonard Dinnerstein et al., Natives and Strangers. Blacks, Indians and Immigrants in America, New York, Oxford University Press, 1990.

9. Maureen Warner-Lewis, Guinea's Other Suns, Dover MA, The Majority Press, 1991.

10. Ibid., pp.98-101.

11. Ibid., pp.144-47.

Racist Ideologies

STEPHEN SMALL

I am apt to suspect the negroes and in general all other species of men, to be naturally inferior to the whites. There never was a civilised nation of any complexion than white nor even any individual eminent in action of speculation. No ingenious manufacturer among them, no arts, no sciences. There are negro slaves dispersed all over Europe of which none ever displayed any symptoms of ingenuity.
(David Hume, 1734)[1]

Vices the most notorious seem to be the portion of this unhappy race; idleness, treachery, revenge, cruelty, impudence, stealing, lying, profanity, debauchery, nastiness and intemperance, are said to have extinguished the principles of natural law, and to have silenced the reproofs of conscience. They are strangers to every sentiment of compassion and are an aweful example of the corruption of man left to himself.
(*Encyclopaedia Britannica*, 1810, vol. XIV, p. 750)[2]

.... there is a physical difference between the white and black races which I believe will forever forbid the two races living together on terms of social and political equality. And inasmuch as they cannot so live, while they do remain together there must be the position of superior and inferior, and I as much as any other man am in favor of having the superior position assigned to the white race.
(Abraham Lincoln, 1858)[3]

Definitions of 'racism'

'Racism' has been defined in a number of different ways. In the past most discussions focused on the development by Europeans of ideologies that argued Africans and Europeans were separate 'races', endowed with different physical and mental attributes, and that Europeans were superior and Africans inferior. The accepted scientific view today dates from a UNESCO statement of the 1940s: 'Racism falsely claims that there is a scientific basis for arranging groups hierarchically in terms of psychological and cultural characteristics that are immutable and innate'.[4] One of the problems with discussions of 'racism' is that some people use the term to refer to the content of an ideology (regardless of any actions that do or do not follow); others mean it to refer to the intentions of individuals or groups; still others refer to the outcomes of actions, intended or otherwise (as in institutional racisms); still others use it to mean all of these. For example, the Institute of Race Relations declares: 'Racialism refers to prejudiced beliefs and behaviour but when these become fully systematised into a philosophy of 'race' superiority, and when this then becomes a part of the way in which society as a whole is organised, then we use the term racism. An individual who acts in a racially prejudiced way is a racialist; a society whose most powerful economic and social institutions – industry, law, media, government – are organised on, or in effect act on, the principle that one 'race' is superior to another is racist.'[5]

A second problem is that there has often been a futile search for the origin of 'racism', a search that suggests that there is a single 'racism' with a single origin. This is characteristic of the view that 'racism' began with slavery in the Americas. This notion has now been discredited and it is clearly better to conceptualise different 'racisms', and to recognise that ideologies can reflect different 'racist' assumptions.

Another complicating factor is the idea that 'racism' is simply one form of ethnocentrism and that ethnocentrism has occurred in all societies at all times. This suggests that it is just another incidence of ethnocentrism and thus no better and no worse than other ethnocentrisms. This neglects the way in which racism towards Africans during slavery has been both more pernicious and lasting in its effects. This 'racism' is inextricably intertwined with financial accumulation, economic expansion, industrial acquisition and the rise and development of capitalism; the international contours of economic, political and social instability reflected in present-day world trade; the enduring effects of racial group barriers, boundaries and identities in the colonial and post-colonial world; the creation of current nation states (both inside and outside Europe) and current national configurations and conflicts in Africa; advances in science which were seized upon to 'justify' oppression and exploitation and injustice; mass voluntary and enforced migrations that populated (and depopulated) the Americas, and has led to the Diasporic presence throughout Europe; the realities of citizenship and non-citizenship, and the extension or denial of the inalienable right to life, liberty and the pursuit of happiness; the cultures and communities of African resistance, from the advocates and practitioners of black Nationalism to those of Pan Africanism, including Martin Delany, Marcus Garvey, W.E.B. Dubois and Kwame Nkrumah.

The enduring effects of 'racism' today are unique to the Atlantic slave era and its effects are almost palpable across the world. This makes it more significant and widespread and its impact more immediate.

Historical changes in ideas about 'race'

It is a mistake to assume that 'racisms' were constant over time, or in different places at the same time. Most of the evidence indicates that early European views of Africans were articulated in religious rather than 'racial' terms. Over time, particularly as slavery became entrenched and was presumed indispensable to European needs, the language of 'racism' became more and more explicit. Winthrop Jordan[6] has documented the changing language used to refer to people from Europe and Africa. The first English to 'settle' in North America called themselves 'Christians' and called Africans 'Negroes'. In the middle of the seventeenth century they increasingly called themselves 'English' and 'free'; after the 1680s they called themselves 'white'.

Banton[7] has shown the development of the language of 'race' both in Europe and in the Americas and he argues that there is no evidence that the word 'race' was used at all in the Americas to differentiate Europeans and Africans until after 1776. The word first appeared in Europe before any contact with Africans, and it referred to lineage, or likeness, without any notion of biological immutability. Relationships of superiority and inferiority are only implied, or are articulated around cultural not biological difference. Thus one has the Irish race, English race and so on. At this time, the word simply refers to a group with common origins. This remained the primary meaning of the word during the sixteenth, seventeenth and eighteenth centuries, and in its applications to Europeans.

As contacts with Africans persisted, most European scientists and middle-class Europeans came to believe that there were three basic races – Caucasoids, Negroids and Mongoloids. While European and (white) American scientists differed greatly on the number of races, they all shared the common (and mistaken) assumption that distinct and unequal races existed. The common mistakes and futility of it all are summed up by Gossett: 'Linnaeus had found four human races; Blumenbach had five; Cuvier had three; John Hunter had seven; Burke had sixty-three; Pickering had eleven; Viry had two "species", each containing three races; Haeckel had thirty-six; Huxley had four; Topinard had nineteen under three headings; Desmoulins had sixteen "species"; Deniker had seventeen races and thirty types.'[8] For some scientists, 'the idea of race was so real that no amount of failure could convince them that it might be an illusion'.[9]

Numerous European and European-American scientists claimed to offer scientific evidence about racial difference, including many of the most nota-ble and eminent scholars of their day. Their work is usually called 'scientific racism'. They include (in the eighteenth century) George Louis Leclerc Buffon and Johan Friedrich Blumenbach in Europe, Dr Charles White in England, and the Reverend Smith in the United States; and (in the nineteenth century) James Cowles Prichard in England, Baron Cuvier and Geoffroy Saint-Hilaire in France, Dr Samuel George Morton, Josiah Clark Nott and George Robin Gliddon in the United States. Blumenbach is responsible for the division of the races into Caucasian, Mongolian, Ethiopian, American and Malay, corresponding to white, yellow, black, red and brown. He may have coined the word 'Caucasian' to mean whites.[10]

When Darwin wrote his *Origins of Species* he fundamentally changed the scientific basis for thinking about race and race differences. But though European scientists eventually accepted his arguments about the basis of human differentiation – that there were multiple overlapping differences between humans, with as many differences within presumed races as between them – they simply modified their racism to suit these new findings.

It is usually assumed that the conclusions of 'scientific racism' were based on the best systematic scientific principles at the time. This is where there is confusion with the idea of 'pseudo-science', 'science' referring to established and accepted principles of the academy, 'pseudo-science' referring to rejected and unacceptable principles. It has become clear that much of the evidence was deliberately distorted and conflicting evidence was ignored. Similarly, the evidence was unconsciously distorted as a result of the unquestioned assumption that European culture was unassailably superior to all others. In any case, Blumenbach's characterization of whites as Caucasian – a classification which still stands even today in the United States and Britain – is based on the observation of a single skull.[11]

Despite proclaiming objectivity, impartiality and openness to all evidence and views, it is clear that none of the dominant studies of racism invited or allowed Africans to offer scientific contributions.

Ideologies of race and gender

While racisms were applied to all Africans, it is clear that distinctions were drawn between men and women as objects of exploitation and manipulation. Europeans were obsessed with African sexuality from the start and different ideologies were developed about African men and African women. Black men were seen as rapists to be lynched and black women as sexual objects to be raped. These ideologies reflected and reinforced the power of gender relations within the white population. All of this served to justify (in Europeans' minds, especially men) their own desires, anxieties and frustrations. It helped ease the conscience of Europeans about breeding, using black men as 'studs', as well as about raping and abusing African women.

In general, 'Whites viewed white women as chaste and pure, charged with the task of ensuring that white men remained "civilized", while whites saw black women as natural whores who enticed white men into sexual relationships'.[12] Davis maintained the central facet of domination was pragmatism: 'Expediency governed the slave holders' posture toward female slaves: when it was profitable to exploit them as if they were men, they were regarded, in effect, as genderless, but when they could be exploited, punished and repressed in ways suited only for women, they were locked into their exclusively female roles.'[13]

Women thus worked in slave fields, in coal mines, in iron foundries or as lumberjacks and ditch-diggers. Nor did pregnancy exempt them from such work.

During slavery 'black women's bodies were ... the playing fields where racism and sexuality converged. Rape as both right and rite of the white male dominating group was a cultural norm'.[14] Furthermore, 'rape was a weapon of domination, a weapon of repression, whose covert goal was to extinguish slave women's will to resist, and in the process, to demoralize their men'.[15] And yet this convergence is the least researched, even in the 1990s, of all the areas of slavery. Consequently, says hooks, there are no books on the

Fig.24
'The execution of a slave, Surinam, 1792' from J. G. Stedman, *Narrative of a five year expedition against the Revolted Negroes of Surinam, 1772-77*, London 1796
Slaves were often forced to inflict punishment on one another and such images helped to reinforce European racial prejudices. Here a free carpenter named Neptune is being executed for killing an overseer.

'sexual sado-masochism of the master who forced his wife to sleep on the floor as he nightly raped a black woman in bed'.[16] This sexual abuse has always been all but glossed over in most literature.[17]

Benign racism

We should not assume pro-slavery whites were all racists and abolitionists were all anti-racist. For example, many slave masters believed blacks were human but they were not prepared to forego their profits from slavery, while many abolitionists believed slavery was evil, that blacks were human, but they were not prepared to interact with them on a social level of equality, certainly not in the area of sexual relations and marriage. None doubted that whites were superior.

Some white abolitionists felt sorrow for Africans, others saw them as the means to rectify the impurities in the white 'race'. For example, many felt that Africans had greater 'religious tendencies', greater 'strength of attachment' and 'gentility' from which the whites could learn. Such benevolent reformers, even romantics, 'tended to see the Negro more as a symbol than as a person, more as a vehicle for romantic social criticism than as a human being with the normal range of virtues and vices'.[18] An example is William Ellery Channing, a moderate anti-slavery writer, who in *Slavery* of 1835 argued 'the African is so affectionate, imitative, and docile that in favourable circumstances he catches much that is good; and accordingly the influence of a wise and kind master will be seen in the very countenance of his slaves'.[19]

Furthermore, many abolitionists refused to let black children into their schools, or to employ blacks except as menials. Some claimed this was dictated by the pressures of the times, but for many it revealed clear antipathies.

A major dispute about the roles of black people in the abolitionist movement in the United States led Frederick Douglass to campaign on his own. White abolitionists had paraded Douglass in front of northern audiences as an example of the adverse effects of slavery on black people. They encouraged him to stutter, act dazed and roll his eyes. But despite being enslaved, Douglass was an accomplished intellect and orator. Fed up of acting out the role of a poor pathetic ex-slave he wanted to contribute more intellectually and analytically to the movement. He was strongly dissuaded and for him, enough was enough. He began to campaign independently of white abolitionists.

Influences on 'racist' attitudes

In general, 'racist' ideas reveal more about the motives and insecurities of whites than about the characteristics or attributes of blacks. A combination of material interests (economic, political and psychological) as well as cultural beliefs gave rise to 'racist' beliefs. Some analysts see such beliefs arising from religious convictions – the idea that blacks were the descendants of Ham described in the Bible. In this conception Christians were simply bringing heathens to be saved in the bosom of the Lord, and slavery was represented as a 'rescue mission'.

Other analysts believe that 'racism' arose from exaggeration and myth about Africa and Africans that were enslaved. For example, stories, tales and caricatures about Africa and Africans were available, or could be interpreted, from the Bible, classical and medieval accounts – *Mandeville's Tales* was a prime example. From the 1570s there was 'an outpouring of literature on Africa'.[20] These accounts described the geography, people, animals and climate of Africa in a colourful and bizarre style such that 'fact and fiction became inextricably fused'.[21] Many such tales were clearly distorted and exaggerated to enhance the stature of the person telling them to audiences that were usually illiterate and gullible. The importance of these early tales is that they set the backdrop for all future understanding of Africa and 'truth fed the expansion rather than the expulsion of mythology, and rumour unshakably fastened itself on reality'.[22]

For still others, 'racist' beliefs arose from personal experience and familiarity with Africans as subordinates. This was the case throughout the Americas for slave masters and non-slave-holding whites. Having forced Africans into slavery, having imposed inferiority by denying them means or motivation to read and write, and having established a system whereby all values, traditions, achievements and accomplishments were to be judged by European values and morality, there was little that the African could do not to be inferior, at least, in the eyes of Europeans. This is clearly tied in with 'racism' as cultural arrogance.

One of the main explanations for the origin and growth of 'racist' ideas is the view that they arose primarily from the economic and political needs of Europeans, especially those with power, who sought to maximise the profits from the colonisation of the Americas. Most notable is the contention of Eric Williams that 'slavery was not born of racism: rather, racism was the consequence of slavery'; and that the reason for slavery 'was economic, not racial; it had to do not with the colour of the labourer, but the cheapness of the labour'. Williams demonstrated how working-class whites, Native Americans and others were first used as sources of labour, but that Africans were identified as being economically cheaper, available in greater numbers and with less (military) repercussions for the Europeans.[23] Over time, the fact that Africans were overwhelmingly slaves gave a 'racial twist' to slavery, and Europeans came to assume that it was the 'natural' position for Africans. This is a view shared by Walvin: 'The first wave of white expansion into Africa ... was conceived in the commercial dreams of European speculators and born of shrewd investment' rather than being about religious liberation.[24]

There is evidence to show that all these sources exercised some impact on 'racist' views. Sometimes it is clear that one particular source was more important than others, though it was often the case that many different sources came together. It seems unlikely that one source alone was the primary force at all times, and it is thus better to ask when and where each source was important, and for which groups. Miles has argued that, though many of these influences were significant, they all became secondary to the economic and political motivations of the dominant

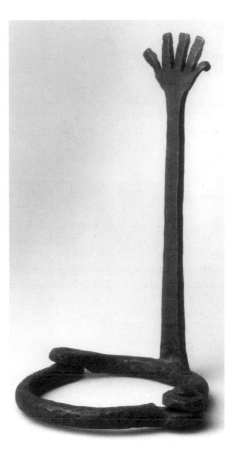

138
Punishment collar
Wrought iron, 18th century

groups in the European nations.[25] As the fortunes and prosperity of the European nations became so intertwined with the exploitation of Africa and the Americas, the issue of whether, in truth, black people were inferior or not became almost irrelevant. The belief in their inferiority by Europeans suited their economic and political pursuits; if it had been advantageous to believe they were equal or even superior, then Europeans would have adjusted their beliefs. In fact they did, for it was clearly believed that Africans were superior workers.

Working-class whites accepted 'racist' views because it supported them psychologically and it provided economic incentives. It enabled them to feel superior to someone, and it left them with the possibility of becoming slave masters themselves some day. Thus a Georgia song popular among working-class whites runs: 'All I need in this creation is a pretty little wife and a slave plantation'.

1. Peter Fryer, *Staying Power: The History of Black People in Britain*, London, Pluto Press, 1987.

2. James Walvin, *Black and White: The Negro and English Society, 1555-1945*, London, Allen Lane, 1973.

3. Michael Banton, *The Idea of Race*, London, Tavistock, 1977.

4. Ashley Montagu, *Statement on Race*, London, Oxford University Press, 1972, p.158.

5. Institute of Race Relations, *Patterns of Racism*, London 1982, p.28.

6. Winthrop Jordan, *White Over Black. American Attitudes Toward the Negro, 1550-1812*, New York, W.W. Norton and Co., 1968.

7. Banton, *op. cit.*

8. Thomas Gossett, *"Race". The History of an Idea in America*, Schocken 1965, p.82.

9. *Ibid.*, p.83.

10. *Ibid.*, p.37.

11. *Ibid.*, p.38.

12. Theresa L. Amott and Julie A. Mattei, *Race, Gender and Work*, Boston, South End Press, 1991.

13. Angela Davis, *Women, Race and Class*, The Women's Press, 1981, p.6.

14. bell hooks, *Yearning. Race, Gender and Cultural Politics*, Boston, South End Press, 1990, p.57.

15. Davis, *op.cit.*, p.24.

16. hooks, *op.cit.*, p.57.

17. Davis, *op.cit.*, p.25.

18. George Stocking, *Race, Culture and Evolution*, New York, Free Press, 1968, p.109.

19. *Ibid.*, p.103.

20. Walvin, *op.cit.*, p.22.

21. *Ibid.*, p.5.

22. *Ibid.*, p.6.

23. Eric Williams, *Capitalism and Slavery*, North Carolina 1944.

24. Walvin, *op.cit.*, p.16.

25. Robert Miles, *Racism and Migrant Labour*, London, Routledge, 1982; *idem, Racism*, London, Routledge, 1989.

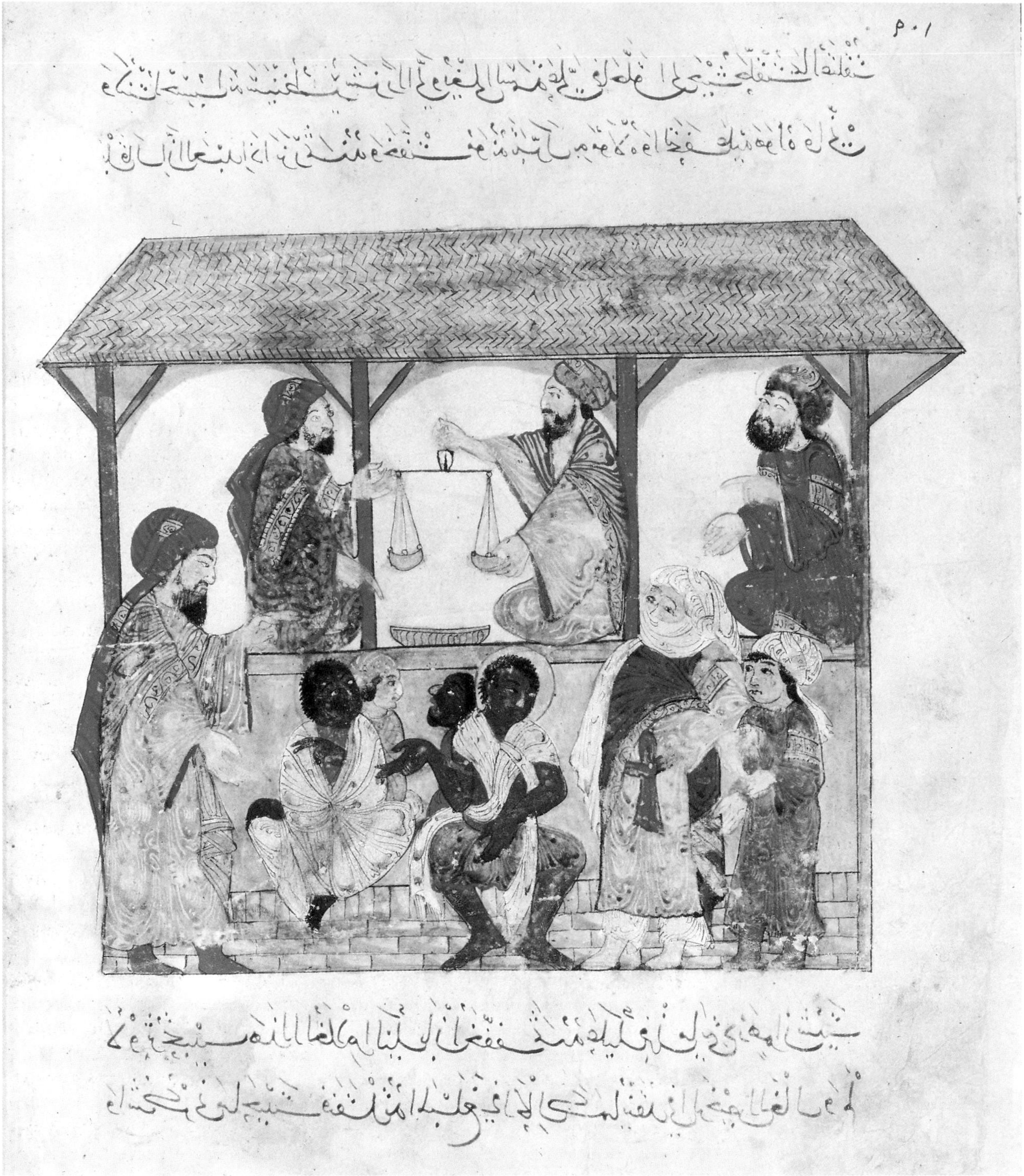

Fig.25
A slave market in Zabid, Yemen, 1237
Slaves were bought and sold in the markets of the Middle East for centuries.

On the Meaning and History of Slavery

PRESTON KING

What does 'slavery' mean?

Slavery always involves compelling some to work for others. But it comes in many forms and degrees. It is very broadly conceived when used to cover any form of compulsory labour. It is more commonly conceived narrowly, to cover only those workers denied all legal or civic rights. The actual conditions of life and work for slaves, however expressed in law, vary in important ways from one town or region or country to another.

What are the different forms of slavery?

Scholars vary in their approaches. There are many different classificatory schemes, no one of which is really adequate. Below, I recommend a rough working distinction between comprehensive and restrictive meanings of slavery.

1. Slavery, in the comprehensive sense, may be taken to involve compulsory labour of any kind – whether for a specific purpose (perhaps to drain a swamp), or for a fixed term (perhaps for five years, after which liberty is restored), or for a recurrent duty (perhaps to reap a harvest on behalf of another). Thus conceived, slavery may refer to such diverse arrangements as Russian serfdom, European medieval villeinage and Spartan helotry (the tenant is tied to the land); the Ottoman janissary corps (Turkish infantrymen, of the four teenth to nineteenth centuries, compelled to serve for life); English 'statutory service' (forcing the poor in the 1sixteenth and seventeenth centuries to submit and work for domestic masters);[1] impressment into the army; 'shanghai-ing' into the navy; compulsory transportation (as to seventeenth-century Virginia and eighteenth-century Australia); convict labour (as in pre-1776 Georgia, in post-1788 New South Wales, in the Soviet 'Gulag Archipelago' and widespread everywhere); 'chain-gang' labour (as in the twentieth-century U.S. South); indentured labour (as of East Indians to Guyana, Trinidad and Fiji in the nineteenth century); child labour (as in so much of the carpet industry in India, Bangladesh and Pakistan); and child prostitution (as currently in Thailand, the Philippines and elsewhere). All of these are cases of unfree, dependent or compulsory labour.

2. Slavery is more commonly conceived in the restrictive sense, involving compulsory labour which is unrelieved by any legal restrictions on the owner of the worker. The work imposed need not answer to any limitations relating to its conditions or duration or type. The circumstance of being deprived of all formal rights, of being reduced in law to an item of property, is also known as 'chattel' slavery. This was the form of enslavement characteristically imposed upon Africans by Europeans in the transatlantic slaving that began in the fifteenth century. At the extreme, the chattel slave can be bought and sold, removed from the land, from husband or wife, from parent or child. He or she can be made to work in the house or in the fields, in company or isolation, to produce goods or provide services, including sexual services. The chattel can be punished in such degree as the master wishes, up to and including death. Whatever the chattel produces (including offspring) is the property of his or her master, since this slave, in law, has neither title to possessions nor rightful access to dependents or relations. Historically, chattel slavery is met with only rarely. As one writer has observed: 'There has seldom been in history ... any slave-holding community in which the theoretical slave – that is, a thing totally devoid of legal personality and without possessions of his own – has really existed in the actual practice of that community. Only in the confinement of prisons can men be totally deprived of all their freedoms, and hence totally enslaved'.[2]

Chattel slavery, however, is more frequently encountered in large-scale states and empires than in smaller entities. It also assumes its most extreme forms, paradoxically, under the most technologically advanced systems. In brief, chattel slavery, if at first rare, became the slavery of choice for modernity and it was unquestionably harsher, more encompassing and more destructive than ever it proved in antiquity.

Europe, in the modern era – from 1492 – opened with, built upon, and persisted in imposing this form of subjection upon Native Americans and Africans for upwards of four hundred years. The harshness of transatlantic slavery went hand in hand with the racist sentiments that came to legitimate this traffic. To treat a people with systematic inhumanity depends upon a capacity to break psychic contact with them as fellow humans. Modern slavery was most extreme, precisely because it was comprehensively racist.[3]

How old is slavery?

Slavery, in its comprehensive forms, may be as old as the earliest of states. Evidence for humans 'owning' one another is apparent from Egyptian tomb inscriptions dating back five thousand years. It is recorded in the poet Homer, writing in the eighth century BC. It is not less prevalent in the Old Testament texts. Yet the type, scale and intensity of slavery is not historically uniform: it waxes and wanes over time. What is clear, however, is the close historical association between the expansion of empire and war, and the extension and worsening of slavery. Early states not only engaged in war for sport, but equally and more importantly, to secure territory, subjects and slaves. Chattel slavery is rare – if we take account of the last six to ten thousand years of human history – but it is not new. The chattel slavery of ancient Greece differed from that of ancient Rome. This differed in turn from that of nineteenth-century Jamaica and Mississippi. Within the Americas, chattel slavery varied from one island or territory or state to the next. Even on the same plantation, the difference in conditions between, for example, the life of 'field slaves' and 'house slaves' could be profound.

There are two constants nonetheless to be remarked. First, the chattel slavery of the Americas was more oppressive than that of ancient Rome, and this more oppressive than that of ancient Greece. Second, the chattel slavery of the American hemisphere absorbed absolutely larger numbers of victims than

did Rome, and Rome more than Greece. So chattel slavery, up to little more than a century ago, was both more extensive and oppressive, in the absolute numbers affected, than ever it was in earlier times. This must raise a large question mark over the character of modernity as a preponderantly progressive era.

What was transatlantic slaving?

This was chattel slavery in its most modern, and almost certainly its worst form. It was begun in the fifteenth century, and ended only in the second half of the nineteenth century – in some cases still later. Even when transatlantic slaving was outlawed, slavery in the Americas continued as before. Even when transatlantic slaving was ended legally, the traffic continued illegally. The conditions of the Atlantic passage were made still worse, in view of the smaller, faster ships, and the closer confinement of victims that they produced. The threat to life was much increased, since ships at risk of being seized would throw their African contraband into the sea to destroy the evidence of their law-breaking.

In the Americas, Columbus took the first Amerindian captives. The effect cumulatively upon native Americans was devastating. In the Caribbean, Amerindians were soon displaced by African captives. The traffic became so enveloping and profitable that the literature still tends to refer to this massacre of the innocents as a trade – 'the African slave trade'. The victims were taken from their native continent on European vessels, transported to the Americas, compelled to work in mines, on farms, the product being exported in turn to Europe.

Did slavery exist in West Africa prior to the arrival of Europeans?

Slavery probably existed in some form in all pre-industrial systems. Certainly it was exploited under all early industrial systems, as in the colonial appendages of Holland, England and France, where chattel slavery was the rule. The

question, then, is not, broadly, whether there was slavery in West Africa, but specifically whether a system of chattel slavery was to be found there.

The short answer is 'no'. This answer may be given without qualification for the fifteenth century, but not after we enter the nineteenth century. Slavery was first introduced by force from European vessels upon the tiny village states of the West African forest zone. These states had, and could have, no sense of a common African identity – no more than did Europeans among themselves. The Africans had petty wars among themselves, which normally did not last long, nor do great damage, simply because there were not the surpluses or resources to fuel them. They did not raid one another for slaves because their semi-subsistence economies were not yet elaborate enough to absorb and discipline such labour. The original, small states of the West African forest zone had no capacity to sustain chattel slavery. Thanks to the tsetse fly infestation, they were not subject to significant horse-borne attack from the savannah empires to their north. Nor, before the fifteenth century, had they been vulnerable to attack from the Atlantic. Rulers in this setting had rather few subjects, controlled tiny areas, and were much given to consultation, especially among elders. They could not commonly afford anything quite so grand as 'war', nor be well placed to maintain many individuals, let alone entire populations, as chattels. The Europeans, who came to this coast in ships, were in a position of significant military strength vis-à-vis the Africans whom they encountered, an advantage they compulsively exploited. We simply do not know when slaving began across the Sahara or in East Africa. We do know that there is no evidence for the claim that it existed 'from time immemorial'. As for the Atlantic coast of West Africa, the direct evidence supplied by the Portuguese is that they began the slaving there, not by buying captives, but by kidnapping victims, and by mounting and then sponsoring wars.

Some apologists for European slaving, as Professor Vincent Thompson has archly observed, have been disposed to

Mannier Hoe de Gevange Kristen Slaven tot Algiers verkoft worden.

Fig.26
A slave market in Algiers, Dutch engraving, 1684
Africans were also traded across the Sahara and were sold throughout North Africa.

give 'the impression that (West) Africans themselves started the slave trade, encouraged it, and refused to put an end to it when a benevolent and humanitarian Europe decided that it was time to call a halt'.[4] It makes rather more sense to assume that considerable psychic distance is required for one group to be able to visit upon another such extreme forms of inhumane treatment. The evolving behaviour of the Portuguese towards, for example, the kingdom of the Kongo (contemporary Angola), from the fifteenth into the sixteenth centuries, from a rough egalitarianism into an utterly destructive exploitativeness, is perfectly consistent with the emergence of such psychic distance. Inhumane behaviour, like that of German Nazis towards Jews and Gypsies (1933-1945), will serve as a reliable marker for extreme racist or ethnocentric attitudes and premises. Similar attitudes would appear to have been essential to justify the reduction of Kongolese and other Africans to the status of chattels for sale in Europe and in the Americas. The Portuguese were followed in their slaving and fomenting of war in West Africa by many other European nations. John Hawkins, Francis Drake, Walter Raleigh were all slavers, and given to piracy – enslaving Africans and robbing Spaniards. Hawkins, as late as 1562-63, tells of leading two hundred of his men ashore in West Africa – with still drummer, and muffled oar, a strict silence enjoined upon all. This was done in the 'hope that they might surprise a village that Hawkins believed to exist some miles up-country, and capture the inhabitants at daybreak before they had risen from sleep'. Hawkins, like others before and after, learned a more efficient way of pursuing his business. This consisted in locating two small states either at or on the verge of a fight, and throwing his powder and shot to the side of one, thus ensuring victory for his allies and virtually all male captives for himself. These captives were forcibly transported into what for them was a 'New World', and their sale produced for Hawkins a considerable fortune.[5] The Portuguese and other Europeans entered into African slaving determinedly only after their discovery and conquest of the Americas supplied a profitable reason for doing so. Many coastal African statelets sought to escape harm, and to enhance their strength, by entering into alliances with the men from the ships. The balance of power shifted away, quite suddenly, from those societies without, to those with, the backing of European arms. Virtually all West African states thus came directly or indirectly under the tutelage of a shifting succession of European nations. The Europeans, starting with the Portuguese, built their forts and castles in impregnable positions – impregnable at least to attack by land. Africans loyal to them could shelter under the walls of these structures. These Africans could aid the Europeans by supplying slaves, or themselves fall victim to the traffic. Over time, larger and more independent West African states evolved, such as Asante, Dahomey, Oyo and Benin. If they had direct access to the sea, as had Benin, then a firm European dependency was imperative, as in Benin's alliance with the Portuguese. If there was no direct European dependency, then the state – like Asante – would materialise deeper within the forest zone, or even (like Oyo) to the north of the forest, and so more immune to attack from seaward. West African coastal states had little choice but to side with, even while victimised by, Euro-

13
Ceremonial sword
Asante, Ghana 19th century

18
Anklet
Ivory, West Africa, (?)18th century

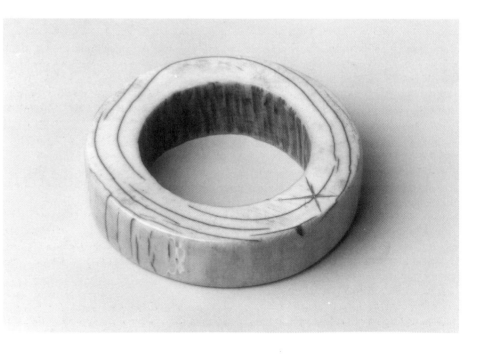

pean slavers. Over the decades and centuries, Africans were pulled more and more deeply into administering a system of kidnapping, raids and war which proved systematically destructive of their societies. The early states along the coast, including the very largest and most flourishing of them – Kongo – were torn apart by the 'trade'. Attempts by African rulers to reject, and later to temper, this slaving were consistently repudiated by the European powers in place. This was true very early in the history of African enslavement, as in the case of King Afonso of the Kongo in the sixteenth century,[6] and very late, as in the case of King Troudo of Dahomey in the eighteenth century.[7]

Conclusion

Slavery, generally, emerged hand in hand with government itself. At a time when machinery was rudimentary, human labour was invaluable. War bred slavery. And the value of slaves fomented war. The resources of early states, however, were too paltry to permit practices even vaguely approximating to unlimited war. The division of labour in such entities being so little advanced, the absorption of only the smallest numbers of slaves was feasible. There were not sufficient tasks to give slaves, nor sufficient resources and technology to repress them. Early slavery was systematically more benign, involved more females than males, and was overwhelmingly domestic in character. With technological advance, up to and including early industrialisation in

our own era, slavery became more pathological and regimented, more impersonal and repressive, more global and culturally imperious. Under the chattel regimes of the modern era, the gender selection and racial indifference of the ancient world were reversed. Thus, male victims were markedly more numerous than female. And victims were overwhelmingly more commonly selected by race than by condition or class or national origin. Those who were most distinct in appearance – Africans, then Indians – were those who became most comprehensively victimised. Transatlantic chattel slavery was imposed by Europeans upon the Africans of the Atlantic coast from the fifteenth century. It was sustained for over four hundred years, until replaced by systems of colonial tutelage, which themselves commonly resorted to forced African labour. The termination of transatlantic slaving did not terminate slaving as such. For, first, the traffic simply became clandestine. Secondly, the system of slavery itself was not affected, being deeply rooted on both sides of the Atlantic by the nineteenth century. Thirdly, when the system of slavery was itself abolished, various measures were introduced to maintain the state of dependency of the new freedmen, including the introduction into the Americas and elsewhere of bondsmen or indentured labourers from Asia.[8]

1. In 1572, an act was passed 'for the punishment of Vagabonds and for the Relief of the Poor and Impotent'. It provided for all 'convicted vagabonds above the age of 14 to be whipped and burned through the right ear unless some honest person takes them into service'. An ablebodied person who had no land or money, and was located in or about any large town, was under severe compulsion to submit to a master of some kind. See, for example, A.L. Beir, *The Problem of the Poor in Tudor and Early Stuart England*, London, Methuen, 1983, pp. 34 and 40.

2. See W.L. Westermann, 'Slavery and the Elements of Freedom in Ancient Greece', in M.I. Finlay (ed.), *Slavery in Classical Antiquity*, Cambridge, W. Heffer & Sons, 1960, p.18.

3. Some of the many books which touch on this question are Thomas Gossett, *Race: The History of an Idea in America*, New York, Schocken Books, 1965; W. Jordan, *White over Black*, Chapel Hill, University of North Carolina Press, 1968; and Joel Kovel, *White Racism: A Psychohistory*, New York, Pantheon, 1970.

4. V.B. Thompson, *The Making of the African Diaspora in the Americas: 1441-1900*, London, Longman, 1987, p.70. See also B. Davidson, *Old Africa Rediscovered*, London, Victor Gollancz, 1961, pp.119-20; W. Rodney, *A History of the Upper Guinea Coast, 1545-1880*, Oxford, Clarendon Press, 1970, pp.40, 260-63 and J.Pope Hennessy, *Sins of the Fathers*, London 1970, p.182.

5. R. Unwin, *The Defeat of John Hawkins*, London, Penguin, 1962, p.71f.

6. See J. Duffy, *Portugal in Africa*, London, Penguin, 1962.

7. See John Atkins, *A Voyage to Guinea, Brazil and the West Indies*, London 1737 (2nd edition, reprinted, Frank Cass).

8. See, for example, Hugh Tinker, *A New System of Slavery: The Export of Indian Labour Overseas, 1830-1920*, Oxford, Oxford University Press/Institute of Race Relations, 1977.

The General Legacy of the Atlantic Slave Trade

STEPHEN SMALL

For the last five hundred years the countries of the West have relentlessly exploited Africa and African people. Millions of Africans were murdered, millions more violently kidnapped and enslaved, women raped and brutalised, and African societies totally ransacked. Slavery and colonialism were carried out for the economic enrichment of the West, with the full legal and political sanction of presidents, prime ministers and the Church. It was exploitation of African labour that led to the expansion of industry across Britain, the United States and the world. At the same time, slavery and colonialism created the circumstances which confine Africans and African nations to the worst conditions experienced by any people in the world today. In the light of these facts, where does one begin to evaluate the effects of the Atlantic slave trade in a world in which, almost 190 years after the slave trade was abolished across the British Empire, and over 150 years after slavery was abolished, Africans and the descendants of Africans remain at such a dire institutional disadvantage compared to those who promoted the trade against them? The millions now starving in Africa can trace their plight to slavery and colonialism, and the poverty they experience is worse than in any other area of the globe. Raw materials and natural assets are ravaged from their rightful owners under shallow promises of fair trading and tawdry policies of arms for aid. Political instability continues to plague territories established around the arbitrary and self-serving boundaries imposed by Europeans. Military dictatorships are responsible for some of the desperation that confronts the continent's millions, but even these have often been set up and supported by duplicitous governments of the West.

In South America and the Caribbean, economies remain underdeveloped and stagnant, people occupy shanty-town dwellings and there is inadequate provision for the educational and health needs of children. Transnational companies exploit cheap labour and lax environmental regulation, even using vulnerable populations to off-load tobacco and alcohol, and to dispose of chemical and industrial waste. In those areas exploited and abandoned by the nations which profited from the Atlantic slave trade, economies continue to find that the World Bank, under the total control of Europeans and Americans, is a more powerful dictate of their essential policies than any indigenous head of state. In the United States and across Europe the descendants of Africans struggle to survive violent attacks, systematic racial hostility, and the continued vilification of Africans and 'blackness'. Formal immigration legislation and institutional practices across 'fortress Europe' are designed to keep Africans out; racial hostility constrains their movements within. It is little wonder that Africans and their descendants live a quality of life fundamentally different from that of Europeans and their descendants. No wonder then that Dubois, one of the most unrelenting advocates of equality for Africa and Africans, could predict in 1903: 'The problem of the twentieth century is the problem of the colour line – the relation of the darker to the lighter races of men in Asia and Africa, in America and in the islands of the sea.'

Evaluating the legacy of slavery

There are few who would doubt that slavery has contributed in fundamental ways to the shape of the contemporary world, and to relations between Africa, the Americas and Europe. But having identified some of the links between slavery and current racial inequality, the difficult question is to establish exactly how it contributed. More specifically, to establish patterns and relationships of causality. An evaluation of the legacy of slavery must take as its starting point the present circumstances within which the descendants of slaves, and of slave masters and their families, find themselves. But there is often divergence around this evaluation. Some analysts claim we cannot understand racial inequality in the 1990s without fundamentally appreciating the legacy of slavery in all its effects. For this group, poverty and powerlessness in Africa, South America and the Caribbean, and racial inequality for black people in the west, is a di-

195
BANSHEE
Builders' model, 1863

rect consequence of the Atlantic slave trade, and of the colonial system to which it gave rise. But there are others who say that the causes of current racial inequality, and the factors that perpetuate it, can only be understood in terms of current conditions, current power relations and current conflict. These analysts point to the failed economic and social policies of territories once dominated by Europeans, and to inflexible economies and political dictators. No one has yet established the criteria by which we might establish which is the right or best answer. Not least because the legacy of slavery is still unfolding and new developments affect our evaluation.

In any case, it would be premature at this stage to decide exactly what the full effects have been, or how best to measure them. Their influence continues, and it is far too early for a definitive evaluation of this pestilence of history. At the moment it seem wisest to accept that both past and present conditions have contributed in a myriad of ways, and recognise that the precise influence of each of them is likely to remain beyond our full explanation.

If we are to begin to assess the legacy of the Atlantic slave trade, then we must first appreciate that the collective memory of slavery of Africans and their descendants is vastly different from that of Europeans and their descendants. To most white people, slavery and colonialism are just a distant memory of nothing in particular. For whites, slavery did not last particularly long, its benefits accrued only to a tiny proportion of white people and the evils of slavery are overshadowed by the role played by British abolitionists. In any case, the rise of Western nations, Britain and the United States in particular, as the industrial supremos of the world, is explicable to them simply in terms of English innate genius. Poverty and penury in Africa, and racial inequality in the West, is explained in terms of black inability, incompetence or laziness.

To black people, though, slavery and colonialism reiterate themselves in our everyday lives, and evoke poignant and immediate memories of suffering, brutalisation and terror. For black people, Western nations achieved their industrial growth and economic prosperity on the backs of blacks, abolished slavery primarily for economic reasons, have discriminated against black people ever since, and are unrepentant about any of it. African under-development and racial inequality in the West is understood primarily in terms of racism and the racist hostility of whites. It is these divergent interpretations of the effects of slavery that resulted in so many whites and so few blacks in 1992 celebrating Columbus.

But surely we must conclude that the legacy is not all negative? There are some who focus on the cultural benefits that have arisen from the crossing of cultures to which slavery gave rise – of music, dance, art and cuisine. Certainly such benefits must be celebrated, but only in the context of the continued degradation of Africa and Africans. For every person who celebrated five hundred years of Columbus, there is another who curses Columbus, celebrates five hundred years of resistance, and urges more.

Aspects of the legacy

The enslavement of Africans and the growth and proliferation of European racisms is inextricably intertwined both with the systems of economic, political and social relations which immediately followed its abolition and with the current contours of the international economic, political and social system, and the gross extremes of inequality which characterize it. There were variations from place to place, but many continuities remained. The legacy of slavery is reiterated in the following.

Economic Systems and Population Movements

As advanced industrial capitalist societies based on wage labour and liberal democracy, countries like Britain, the United States, France, Spain, Portugal and the Netherlands have all achieved substantial economic development via conquest, slavery and the exploitation of African labour. It was this labour that fed financial accumulation, economic expansion and the base for industrial acquisition, that is, the development of capitalism.

Central to the international economic system which we now share have been the mass migrations that populated (and depopulated) the Americas – migrations which have led to the Diasporic presence throughout Europe and the Americas.

Racialisation and racist ideologies

'Racialisation' simply means the process by which Africans and Europeans came to be defined as races. This is an historical process born of the contact between the two continents, of the goals of Europeans and of the unequal power relations between the two. It is during slavery and colonialism that racist ideologies were developed and disseminated. The end of slavery saw racist ideologies re-shaped to meet the complex and changing conditions of industrialisation, but with a brutal consistency in their vilification of Africans and insistence of black inferiority.

Racist theories continued to be developed by the most distinguished and respected scientists of Europe and North America, who seized upon science to 'justify' oppression, exploitation and injustice. In the contemporary world, evidence abounds of multiple 'racisms' as the rationalisations used to assert African inferiority have been re-articulated, advocacy of racial hostility has moved from the overt to the covert, and racism has become, in the words of Sivanandan, 'less visible but no less virulent'.

Racist ideologies underlie the enduring effects of racial group barriers, boundaries and identities in the modern world. These ideologies have continued to plague blacks throughout the continent and the Diaspora. There are at least two reasons for this. One is that such ideologies were deliberately modified by whites in the light of post-slavery circumstances. A second reason is that racial identities and antipathies established during slavery set in process institutional practices which continued after slavery ended – for example, those around colour, where conflict has continued at various levels between those of different shades in the black community.

Institutional racist practices

From the *de facto* subordination of Africans across European colonies and apartheid in South Africa, to legal segregation in the United States and discrimination across Europe, institutional racist practices have been central to the creation of modern nation states (both inside and outside Europe) and current conflicts in Africa, South America and the Caribbean. Racist practices also shaped the realities of citizenship and non-citizenship, and the extension or denial of the inalienable right to life, liberty and the pursuit of happiness.

In those nations that promoted slavery, white exclusionary practices continued to operate after its demise – based on notions of biological inferiority here, cultural inferiority there – and systematic racial discrimination has led to the concentration of blacks in the most disadvantaged sections of society. In the 1990s, many whites hold racist views about who qualifies as a full member of the country and community, views which have often become enshrined in institutional form, particularly in immigration legislation. Western nations have thus struggled with the ideals that they espouse and have failed to extend those ideals to Africans and other minorities. So despite lofty ideals of freedom, equality, democracy and fairness, these countries have systematically excluded Africans and their descendants from the benefits of such ideals.

The duplicity of Western governments

Successive governments during and since slavery have continued to play a role in re-articulating racial ideology and in managing the racial crisis, often engaging in conflicting and contradictory methods – denial here, compromise there, defeat elsewhere. Governments have been the prime movers of racist ideologies and practices under apartheid in South Africa, through forced colonial labour across African colonies dominated by the West, through the Supreme Court in the United States and through immigration legislation in Britain and France.

Currently, these governments share a focus on the use of anti-discrimination laws as mechanisms for defusing social conflict and breaking down patterns of disadvantage and discrimination. While relatively strong on paper, such laws have often been limited in practical effect, and the integrity of governments is challenged by the fact that much of their immigration legislation is predicated on racist assumptions. The current attempts to consolidate a 'fortress Europe', white on the inside, Africans and people of colour excluded, or marginalised within, perpetuate the impact of racial hostility.

The colour line

The overarching similarity across these nations, with modifications, is of course the 'colour line' – the inequality between white and black of wealth, income, employment, education, health and housing – which characterizes the African experience. Wealth, affluence and good health are enjoyed overwhelmingly by the majority of the world's population, which is white; while poverty and ill health befall Africans and their descendants.

Communities of resistance

The legacy of slavery has everywhere given rise to sustained response by people of African origin, and to cultures and communities of resistance. Continued injustice and exclusion gave rise to separate, and separatist, groups, organizations and institutions based on notions of autonomy and self-determination for black people. From national and international movements such as black nationalism, Pan-Africanism and Negritude, to black organizations and groups, black individuals and a whole array of nationalist and anti-imperialist movements across the length and breadth of Africa.

For example, in Africa, from Kwame Nkrumah, Jomo Kenyatta and Julius Nyerere to Robert Mugabe, Nelson Mandela and Leopold Senghor. In the Caribbean, from Paul Bogle and George William Gordon to Franz Fanon and Marcus Garvey; from Michael Manley and Maurice Bishop to C.L.R. James. In the United States, from the Negro Academy and the National Association of Colored Women to the Urban League, the Nation of Islam, the Southern Christian Leadership Conference and the Black Panther Party. From Sojourner Truth and Ida B. Wells to Mary Mcloud Bethune and Mary Church Terrell, and

from Rosa Parks to Angela Davis. In Britain, the League of Coloured Peoples, the Campaign Against Racial Discrimination, the West Indian Standing Conference, the Race Today Collective and the Institute of Race Relations. In France, the activities of Leopold Senghor and Aimé Cesaire and Léon-Gotran Dumas. Cultures and communities of resistance have always been international, as links across the Diaspora were established and sustained. Black people have always looked across the Diaspora – and travelled across it – for comfort, support and ideas. Africans, African Americans and African Caribbeans actively travelled to challenge slavery, colonialism and imperialism, and were foremost in the successful national liberation struggles. These advocates of equality and self-determination visited numerous countries to establish the Pan-African Congress, whose meetings were attended by the soon-to-be leaders of African nations - Kwame Nkrumah, Jomo Kenyatta and Julius Nyerere.

Black people in England have also looked abroad for inspiration and encouragement; from Olaudah Equiano and Ottobah Cuguano to Ignatius Sancho – names which should roll off our tongues easily but do not because we are not told about them at school – who played decisive roles in the campaign to abolish the slave trade and slavery. They went beyond our differences to demand and defend the interests of the black community as a whole.

A central concern in such struggles has been the idea, ideal and reality of Africa, as concept and inspiration, perhaps summed up best in Garvey's argument in favour of 'Africa for the Africans, at home and abroad'. One part of Garvey's great mission was to return Diasporic Africans to the continent, but a greater and larger mission was to make Africa a place to which Africans throughout the Diaspora could look with pride and self-respect when oppressed or exploited for being African.

While the efforts of those who were most successful are bound to attract our attention, we must also and always recognise the efforts of those many thousands who struggled without re-

ward, without credit, without fame or fortune, but without whom great leaders would never become great, and without whom not even one per cent of what has been achieved would ever have been achieved.

As the 1990s unfold, resistance remains central in the efforts of people of African origin – and their allies – to come together to contain the worst atrocities of racial injustice, and to establish agendas, priorities, political action and policies to overcome them. Its most current articulation around slavery is reflected in the reparations movement.

Reparations

During the 1990s black people began demanding reparations from the nations of the West for the atrocities, injustice and exploitation perpetrated against Africa and Africans during slavery and colonialism. An international conference took place in Abuja, Nigeria, in April 1993, attended by representatives of the Organisation of African Unity, members of African national governments, and distinguished scholars and lawyers. The Abuja Conference was attended by Bernie Grant, MP for Tottenham, London, who put forward a motion in the House of Commons demanding that the issue of reparations be debated.

In Britain a steering committee was established to co-ordinate activities: Reparations U.K. It demands that Europe and the United States acknowledge the crimes committed during slavery and the benefits they have enjoyed, and pay for what they have done via reparations. Reparations is a legally enforced repayment for the damage and destruction caused. Reparations were made by the German government to Israel for the Jewish victims of the Nazi Holocaust; reparations were made by the United States' government to the Japanese and Japanese Americans interned during World War Two. In other words, a clear legal precedent has been established.

The Reparations movement believes that Europe and the United States must cancel financial debts, or transfer capital, or offer services to those they have victimised, or find some other way of making restitution. They must also return the treasures stolen from African societies, and currently housed in the museums of the West. As a matter of urgency, they must meet with the heads of African nations, and with representatives of African peoples elsewhere, to decide how this can be done.

The Reparations movement believes that its case is morally right, economically sound, politically inevitable, and legally inescapable. But it must convince those who wield the power and economic benefits derived from slavery of the rightness of their case. The Reparations movement believes that all who are committed to justice, and to ensuring that the whole of the world's population benefits from the hard work of past and present generations, must support black people's demands for reparations.

Conclusion

The effects of the Atlantic slave trade are palpable across the world today; they are most prominent in the minds of Africans and their descendants. The particular impact the Atlantic slave trade has had varies from continent to continent, from country to country and within countries. But the consequences of the devastation it caused remain. This makes the European trade in Africans more significant, and its impact more immediate, than any other system of slavery. The question of whether slavery alone caused the present conditions across Africa, or the Americas, or Europe, becomes irrelevant. The key issue is that current contours of racial injustice, hostility and inequality can be traced directly to the Atlantic slave trade, and the memory of slavery remains prominent in the minds of Africa and her children.

The descendants of Africans and of Europeans view the legacy of the slave trade from different vantage points. This is bound to be the case in the immediate future, and we can expect no consensus. Without acknowledgement and action, it could remain the case indefinitely. Africans and Europeans recognise that the changes brought about by the Atlantic slave trade are irreversible. Africans and their descendants realise that there is nothing that the West can ever do to make right the wrongs committed during slavery and colonialism. But they also insist that the West can begin to loosen the shackles of poverty and economic distress which continue to hold back Africans and Africa. It is these obstacles enshrined in the international, economic and political infrastructure of trade, more than anything, which impede the development of Africa and the rights of Africans' descendants. Only by tackling the unfairness of these systems can we begin together to create a more morally acceptable economic and political system within which the world's entire population can prosper.

Catalogue

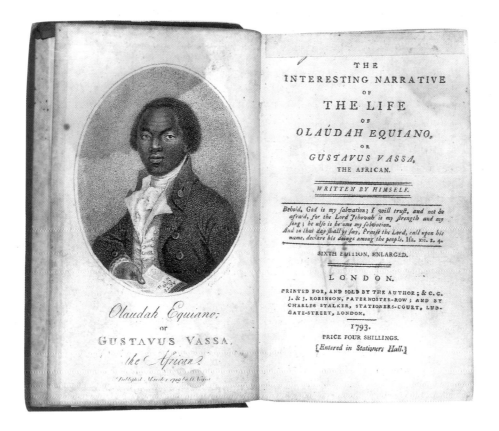

162
'The Interesting Narrative of the life of
Olaudah Equiano, or Gustavus Vassa, the
African. Written by himself'
6th edition, London, 1793

A number of objects in the gallery are on loan from other museums for a limited period of time only. The objects on show may vary slightly from those listed below.

Origins of Transatlantic Slavery

When the Spanish first arrived on the American continent they were dazzled by the abundance of precious metals. Pre-Columbian cultures were rich in finely crafted objects made of gold and silver. Large numbers of these objects were seized and shipped back to Europe, mainly to be melted down. In fact many of the objects were made of tumbaga, an alloy of copper and gold. The Spanish took control of mining production and many of the earliest Africans to arrive in the Americas were put to work in the mines of Central and South America.

3

1 (illus. p. 21)
Part of beaker with face
Silver, Peru
124 × 93 × 130mm
NMGM (Liverpool Museum). N/N 11

2 (illus. p. 26)
Beaker, repoussé decoration of bands with scrolls and birds
Silver, Peru
115 × 105 × 156mm
NMGM (Liverpool Museum). N/N 12

3
Pair of Earrings, each consisting of a hollow ring with attached flat round-shaped shield with repoussé decoration of four jaguars
Gold, Cuenca, Ecuador
192 × 90mm; 196 × 91mm
NMGM (Liverpool Museum). M13034.1-2

4 (illus. p. 28)
Figurine
Tumbaga, Columbia
80 × 67mm
NMGM (Liverpool Museum). N/N 15

5 (illus. p. 22)
Nose ornament
Gold, South America
59 × 40mm
NMGM (Liverpool Museum). N/N 18

6 (illus. p. 17)
Scorpion
Gold, Central South America
30 × 21mm
NMGM (Liverpool Museum). 10.10.78.43

7 (col. illus. p. 19)
Idol, two male figures joined at body
Tumbaga, Mexico
126 × 66mm
NMGM (Liverpool Museum). M13035

8 (illus. p. 22)
Nose ornament
Gold, Columbia
42 × 39mm
NMGM (Liverpool Museum). 24.7.99.144

9 (col. illus. p. 19)
Funerary mask with repoussé facial features
Tumbaga, with vestiges of red paint, Sican culture, Peru, c.900–1500
183 × 305mm
NMGM (Liverpool Museum). N/N 20

10 (illus. p. 28)
Duho
Carved wood, inscription on underside 'This stool was found in a cave in the Island of Eleuthera, Bahamas about the year 1820 by James Thompson a slave and purchased of him by Theo' Pugh Wes.

Miss' in 1835. It is supposed to be either a piece of the domestic furniture of the Indians or one of their Gods. It is at least 300 years old. 1850', Taino, Caribbean
355 × 195 × 115mm
Museum of Mankind. 1918.1

Very few objects survive from the Pre-Columbian civilizations in the Caribbean. The Taino culture of Arawaks was based principally on the island of Hispaniola and parts of Cuba and Puerto Rico.

West African Cultures

West Africa was an area of rich and diverse societies and cultures before and during the era of transatlantic slavery. This is indicated by a small selection of objects. Although the majority date from the 19th century, they use traditional styles which exemplify earlier periods. Music was a vital part of West African life. Although individual music-making was common, music often accompanied dance and had a ceremonial and official role in many communities. A wide variety of drums, wind and stringed instruments existed.

11 (illus. p. 61)
Carving of a woman and child
Carved and painted wood, Lualli River, Cacongo, West Central Africa, 19th century
205 × 163 × 595mm
NMGM (Liverpool Museum). 24.9.00.44

12 (illus. p. 63)
Carving of a woman in a cloth skirt
Carved and painted wood, with (?)printed cotton skirt, Winneba, Ghana, 19th century
135 × 120 × 420mm
NMGM (Liverpool Museum). 13.2.09.25

13 (illus p. 121)
Ceremonial sword
Cast handle with incised decoration terminated in the shape of a human head, and flat blade with incised decoration and animal shape, cut from sheet metal stamped 'A E ???FRITT & SONS', brass, Asante, Ghana, 19th century
600 × 150 × 40mm
NMGM (Liverpool Museum) 10.5.98.1.

The stamped name on the blade indicates that it was manufactured from a sheet of brass, probably exported from Britain in the early 19th century. The general style of decoration is traditional.

14
Stool
Carved wood, Asante, Ghana
470 × 220 × 350mm
NMGM (Liverpool Museum). 1977.297.2

The stool was a symbol of power and authority in Akan cultures and was widely found in both official and domestic usage

15
Prayer board with Arabic inscription
Hausa, Nigeria
450 × 240mm
NMGM (Liverpool Museum). 50.78.179

16 (illus. p. 108)
Comb
Carved wood, Old Calabar, Nigeria
100 × 245mm
NMGM (Liverpool Museum). 16.6.76.24

17 (illus. p. 108)
Robe
Woven indigo-dyed cotton embroidered with white cotton, Hausa, Nigeria
2440 × 1290mm
NMGM (Liverpool Museum). 1252A

14

15

21

23

24

18 (illus. p. 120)
Anklet

Ivory, West Africa, (?)18th century
123 × 125 × 30mm
NMGM (Merseyside Maritime Museum).
1993.137

Although frequently referred to as
'slave anklets' there is no evidence to
establish a particular link with
enslavement. Indeed, the value of
ivory suggests that such ornaments
would have been worn by wealthier
members of society.

19 (illus. p. 62)
Calabash

With inscribed geometrical patterns,
Rabba, Nigeria, 1860
360 × 330 × 170mm
NMGM (Liverpool Museum). 20.11.60.3

20 (illus. p. 62)
Calabash

Painted with geometrical designs in red
and black, Garoua, Cameroon
215 × 190 × 110mm
NMGM (Liverpool Museum). 2.9.1909.20

21
Calabash

Painted with band of geometrical designs
in black, Garoua, Cameroon
215 × 210 × 110mm
NMGM (Liverpool Museum). 2.9.1909.19

22 (illus. p. 109)
Bow lyre

Leather, wood and string, West Africa
200 × 90 × 610mm
NMGM (Liverpool Museum). 7.7.1870.24

23
Gong, of two flattened bell shapes,
joined at top and edges

Wrought iron, Calabar, Nigeria
280 × 230 × 55mm
NMGM (Liverpool Museum). 16.4.61.183

24
Algaita

Wood with tin and reed mouthpiece,
Missan, Nigeria
325 × 85 × 90mm
NMGM (Liverpool Museum). 21.1.1925

25 (illus. p. 109)
Calabash guitar with bow

West Africa
720 × 160 × 190mm; bow 590mm
NMGM (Liverpool Museum). 22.11.24.8

26 (illus. p. 109)
Small drum with drum stick
West Africa
180 (dia) × 315mm; drumstick 280mm
NMGM (Liverpool Museum). 65

27
Small drum
Akim, Accra, Ghana
140 (dia) × 340mm
NMGM (Liverpool Museum). 19.4.98.8

28 (illus. p. 98)
Trumpet
Mande, Gambia
360mm
NMGM (Liverpool Museum). 25.7.89.4

Early European Contact

Europeans were initially drawn to West Africa by the lure of gold. Trading in the metal was begun along the 'Gold Coast' by the Portuguese in the 15th century and was continued by English and Dutch traders in the 16th and 17th centuries. Gold was a central feature of the Asante culture and objects, particularly for adornment were cast by specialised craftsmen using the lost-wax technique.

29 (illus. p. 96)
Plaque showing Bini figures
Brass, Benin, 16/17th century
330 × 380mm
Museum of Mankind. 1898.1-15 no.2

This plaque is evidence of the European presence in West Africa. Although the central figure is a Bini guard in armour, there are representations of Portuguese soldiers and of manillas, one of the main trade goods on either side of his head. The two lower figures with gong and pipes again emphasize the importance of music.

30 (illus. p. 16)
Map of Europe and North Africa
Parchment, 16th century
840 × 570mm
NMGM (Merseyside Maritime Museum). 32.99

31
Three pendants in the form of cowrie shells
Gold, Asante, Ghana
19mm
Museum of Mankind. H.C. Ash 52 A-C

33

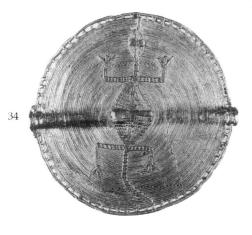

34

35

36

32
Ring
Gold, Asante, Ghana
31mm
Museum of Mankind. 1979 AF1 4661

Gold rings were worn by royal officials on fingers and toes, often several at a time. This ring features three cannon, showing the influence of European armaments.

33
Hollow casting representing three elephants
Gold, Asante, Ghana
84mm
Museum of Mankind. 1900 4-27 44

34
Pectoral disc, repoussé decoration of concentric circles with a stylised salamander
Gold, Asante, Ghana
51mm (dia)
Museum of Mankind. 1900 4-27 36

35
Pectoral disc, repoussé decoration featuring stylised leaves
Gold, Asante, Ghana
90mm (dia)
Museum of Mankind. H.C. Ash 18

36
Pectoral disc, repoussé decoration
Gold, Asante, Ghana
39mm (dia)
NMGM (Liverpool Museum). 10.10.78.45

These discs were worn by young male servants of the Asante king on a cord around their necks. The servants were known as 'souls' and preceded the king on ceremonial occasions to ward off evil. The discs are often known as soul-washers badges.

37 (not illus.)
Sample of gold ore
Quartz conglomerate with pyrites and native gold, Ghana
170mm
NMGM (Liverpool Museum). 1964.316.B

40

Kuduo, bowl with feet, and domed-shaped lid and central handle

Asante, Ghana, 18th century
125 (dia) × 150mm
NMGM (Liverpool Museum). 7.3.05.1

41

Kuduo, rectangular box with lid decorated with geometrical designs and 12 birds

Cast brass, Asante, Ghana, 18th century
77 × 30 × 30mm
NMGM (Liverpool Museum). 16.2.06.39

42

Scales for measuring gold dust, of two circular pans and bar with incised and punched decoration

Brass with plant fibre, Asante, Ghana
bar 120mm; dishes 52mm (dia)
NMGM (Liverpool Museum). 22.10.03.21

43

Three spoons for measuring gold dust

Brass with incised decoration, Asante, Ghana
80mm; 57mm; 135mm
NMGM (Liverpool Museum). 22.10.1903.17-19

38

Kuduo, cylindrical base on cage-shaped stand, lid with loop and handles decorated with birds

Brass, Asante, Ghana, c.1730-49
105 (dia) × 140mm
NMGM (Liverpool Museum). 16.2.06.36

39 (illus. p. 104)

Kuduo, cylindrical base on cage-shaped stand

Brass, Asante, Ghana, c.1730-49
110 (dia) × 95mm
NMGM (Liverpool Museum). 16.2.06.32

42

43

44

44

44

44
Weights
Brass, Asante, Ghana, 17th-19th century
NMGM (Liverpool Museum)
a) representing a box, 37 × 34 × 29mm.
16.2.06.45
b) representing a stool, 50 × 30 × 27mm.
59.94.4
c) rectangular, 16 × 14mm. 15.8.04.36
d) L-shaped, 33 × 32mm. 27.10.03.33

Gold dust was used as a means of exchange in Akan societies from at least the 15th century. The dust was stored in kuduos, which were boxes generally made of brass. Weighing equipment and small brass weights were essential for trading. The weights were produced in large numbers and a variety of designs. The geometrical ones are usually earlier than the figurative ones.

Enslavement

The arrival of Europeans in West Africa brought in its wake a powerful new weapon – the gun. European firearms became an important feature of trade and it is estimated 20 million guns were exported to Africa during the slaving period. They changed the nature of warfare and raiding between different groups and assisted enslavement. Their importance is reflected in their representation in art and their use as a decorative motif.

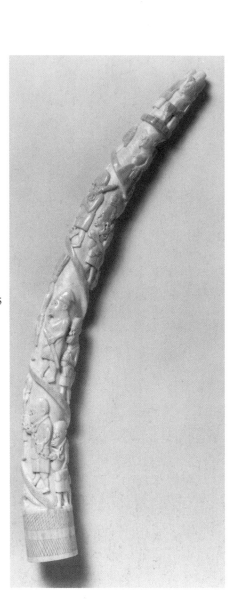

45

45 (colour detail p. 2)
Carved ivory tusk, showing chained figures
Gabon, 19th century
340mm
NMGM (Liverpool Museum). 28.2.27.30

46 (illus. p. 102)
Plaque showing European with gun
Brass, Benin, 16/17th century
170 × 410mm
Museum of Mankind. 1898.1-15 no.11

47 (illus p. 103)
Trade gun, known as a dane gun
18th century
1720mm
Museum of Mankind. 1978 AF22 843

48 (illus. p. 103)
Weights
Brass, Asante, Ghana, c.18th century
NMGM (Liverpool Museum)
a) representing a man with gun, 40 × 28mm. 1974.30.24
b) representing a gun, 65mm. 7.3.05.87
c) representing a cannon, 95 × 20mm. 50.78.354

49 (illus. p. 107)
Yoke
West Africa, 19th century
1745mm
Anti-Slavery International. MH LI 93-4

50 (illus. p. 98)
War trumpet
Ivory, Congo, 19th century
670mm
NMGM (Liverpool Museum). 29.7.1901.2

Trading and Trade Goods

Europeans exported a wide range of items to trade for slaves, often responding to African demands for particular goods. They were mostly manufactured goods with practical applications, like firearms or textiles. Some items, such as cowries and manillas, could be used as currency or others had a decorative function, like beads.

51
Map of West African coast with inset of Goree Island, 'Carte Particuliere / Des Costes de / L'Afrique / Qui comprehend le Royaume de Cacheo le Province de Gelofo etc / Levee Par Ordre Expres des Roys de Portugal sous qui on en a Fait la Decouverte / A Amsterdam / chez Pierre Mortier Libraire /....'
Pierre Mortier, Amsterdam, 1693
395 × 530mm
National Maritime Museum, London. 241 2/1

52 (illus. p. 100)
Map of Congo and Angola, 'Regna / Congo / et / Angola'
John Ogilby, London 1670
330 × 275mm
National Maritime Museum, London. 241 6/1

53 (illus. p. 101)
Map of Africa, printed, coloured, 'Africam Graeci Libyam App: / AFRICAE TABVLA NOVA / Edita Antverpiae 1570'
Probably from Ortelius, *Theatrum Orbis Terrarum*, Antwerp, 1570
480 × 365mm
National Maritime Museum, London. G290 1/10

54 (illus. p. 78)
'An Accurate / MAP of / AFRICA / from the Best / Authorities'
'Engrav'd for the Beauties of Nature and Art display'd. Printed for G. Robinson, in Pater-noster Row, London / V.g.p.139', 18th century
235 × 201mm
NMGM (Merseyside Maritime Museum). 1976.291

55 (illus. p. 15)
Trade token, inscribed 'Tom Buck of Grandy Bonny an Honest Trader he sold me 20 Slaves Ship Liverpool'
Ivory
133mm (dia)
NMGM (Merseyside Maritime Museum). 1961.57

56 (illus. p. 29)
Trade token, inscribed 'JOHN PEPPER BRIG HIGHFIELD A GOOD MAN'
Ivory
95mm (dia)
NMGM (Liverpool Museum). 4427M

The exact significance and use of these tokens have not been established but they were presumably exchanged as pledges or receipts.

57
Two lead-shot bags
Hessian, printed with Royal Coat of Arms 'PATENT SHOT NEWTON, KEATES & Co. LEAD MERCHANTS. LIVERPOOL No.5' and 'No.6'
No.5 281 × 165mm; No.6 265 × 163mm
NMGM (Merseyside Maritime Museum). 1986.201

Arms and ammunition were one of the most important items exported to West Africa, not least because of their impact on the nature of warfare.

58 (illus. p. 30)
Head dress of cowrie shells with roan antelope horns
Kon Kombo, West Africa
580 × 430 × 285mm
NMGM (Liverpool Museum). 56.25.161

59 (illus. p. 31)
String of cowrie shells
West Africa
850mm
NMGM (Liverpool Museum). 11.2.18.11

Cowries came originally from the Maldive Islands in the Indian Ocean and mainly reached Africa on slave ships via Ceylon and Amsterdam. They were used as currency in many areas of West Africa but were also used in decorative ways as a reflection of wealth and position.

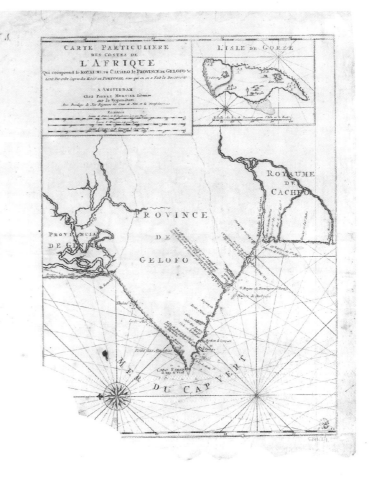

51

57

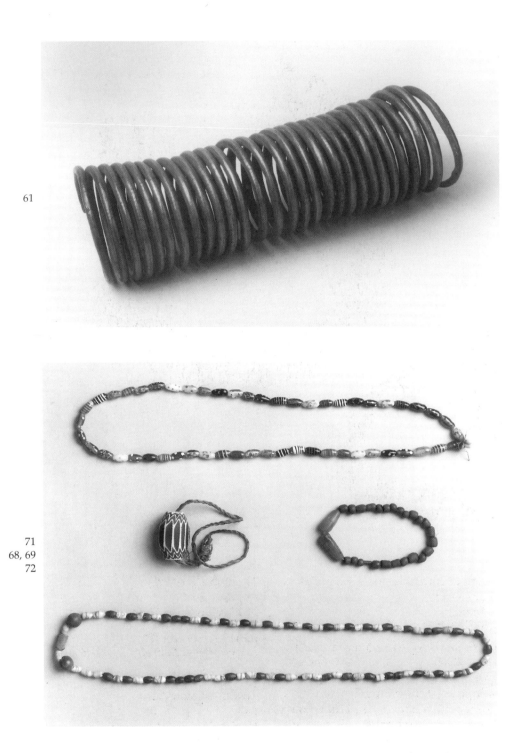

61

71
68, 69
72

60 (illus. p. 31)
Necklace
Hollow tubes of coiled wire, brass, Muni River, Eloby, West Africa
135(dia) × 85mm
NMGM (Liverpool Museum). 19.4.98.55

61
Bracelet
Continous tube of coiled wire, brass, West Africa
80(dia) × 250mm
NMGM (Liverpool Museum). 51.68.738

62 (illus. p. 31)
Gin bottle
Green glass, square sided, with 'v HOYTEMA & C.' moulded in glass, Dutch, 18th century
National Maritime Museum, London

This bottle was found on the New Calabar River, near Iba, in present-day Nigeria. Alcohol was one of the main items exported to West Africa by British and European traders.

63 (col. illus. p. 20)
String of yellow beads with green, red and blue 'tartan' decoration
Glass
255mm
NMGM (Liverpool Museum). 51.68.546

64 (col. illus. p. 20)
String of yellow beads with green, red and blue decoration
Glass, Venetian, from Krobo, Ghana
110mm
NMGM (Liverpool Museum). 51.68.775

65 (col. illus. p. 20)
Yellow bead, with green and red decoration
Glass, from Krobo, Ghana
23mm
NMGM (Liverpool Museum). 1980.108.8

66 (not illus.)
String of clear, white, black, red and green beads with white, yellow and red decoration
Glass
210mm
NMGM (Liverpool Museum). 46.35.54

67 (col. illus. p. 20)
String of beads
Coral, Benin
370mm
NMGM (Liverpool Museum). 42.11

74, 75

68
Bead, white with blue and brown geometrical decoration
Glass, Venetian, from Northern Nigeria
42mm
NMGM (Liverpool Museum). N/N89

69
String of agate, Cambray type, and Indian glass beads from a wreck of a ship off St Agnes, Isles of Scilly
130mm
NMGM (Liverpool Museum). 1987.9.1-4

70 (col. illus. p. 20)
Trade beads
250mm
NMGM (Liverpool Museum). 1992.05.19

71
Levine beads
Glass, Bethnal Green, London
400mm
NMGM (Liverpool Museum). 56.29.603

72
String of cornaline dialleppo pink and white beads
445mm
NMGM (Liverpool Museum). N/N

Glass beads were a regular cargo. In the 1770s they made up between 25% and 50% of the value of cargoes shipped by the Liverpool merchant William Davenport to the Cameroons. Davenport also supplied other slave traders and in 1766-70 sold beads worth about £39,000. Many beads came from Venice but increasingly they were made in many other parts of Western Europe.

73 (illus. p. 33)
Four queen manillas
Copper
NMGM (Liverpool Museum)
a) 285 × 140mm. 28.3.07.15
b) 270 × 120mm. 28.3.07.16
c) 270 × 120mm. 1991.41.2
d) 235 × 170mm. 26.6.11.23

74
Three small manillas
Copper alloy
NMGM (Liverpool Museum)
a) 60 × 60mm. 46.47
b)106 × 95mm. 32.103.3
c) 100 × 90mm. 32.103.2

75
Two small manillas
Brass
NMGM (Liverpool Museum)
a) 66 × 68mm. 1942.18
b) 60 × 60mm. 1942.18

Manillas are horseshoe-shaped bracelets of brass or copper which were used as a form of currency particularly in the Niger delta. They were manufactured in European foundries and were frequently used as a source of metal for casting in Africa.

139

76 (not illus.)
Clay pipe
English, 18th century
NMGM (Merseyside Maritime Museum)

Clay pipes were exported throughout the slaving period and fragments have been found in many parts of West Africa. They were also no doubt used by resident European traders.

77 (illus. p. 32)
Sample of brocaded silk
c.1770-80
480 × 930mm
NMGM (Liverpool Museum). 1988.20.19.b

Cloth was the largest single item exported to Africa. Fashions in demand varied on different parts of the coast and at different times. Some cloths were standard woollens from England and Flanders, or linens from the Netherlands and Silesia. There was also a significant demand for more luxurious silks and cottons from India. Later, European imitations of Indian cloths were produced.

European Traders

The merchants who organized the slave trade were often prosperous and respected members of their communities. Their activities were regarded as beneficial to their fellow citizens. The ships they used are represented in a number of contemporary art forms which are important documentary sources.

78 (illus. p. 75)
Guinea
Gold, Royal African Company, 1663, obverse, bust of king and elephant, 'CAROLVS II DEI GRATIA', reverse Royal arms, 'MAG BR FRA ET HIB REX 1665'
British Museum. Banks E1528

79
Guinea
Gold, Royal African Company, 1665, obverse, bust of king and elephant, 'CAROLVS II DEI GRATIA', reverse Royal arms, 'MAG BR FRA ET HIB REX 1665'
British Museum. Banks v.1p.75

79

80

80
5 Guineas
Gold, Royal African Company, 1668, obverse, bust of king and elephant, 'CAROLVS II DEI GRATIA', Reverse Royal arms, 'MAG BR FRA ET HIB REX 1668'
British Museum. Grueber 720

81
5 Guineas
Gold, Royal African Company, 1669, obverse, bust of king and elephant, 'CAROLVS II DEI GRATIA', Reverse Royal arms, 'MAG BR FRA ET HIB REX 1669'
British Museum. E1509

The Royal African Company had a monopoly of trade to Africa until 1698. It had the privilege of having coins struck at the mint from metal which it imported. The gold came from Guinea and the name was transferred to the coin.

82 (illus. p. 74)
Thomas Golightly
British School, oil on canvas, 19th century
890 × 692mm
NMGM (Walker Art Gallery). 7001

Thomas Golightly (1732-1821) was a leading Liverpool merchant and civic leader. He was elected to the Council in 1770 and served as Bailiff (1770), Mayor (1772-73) and was a Senior Member and Treasurer (1789-1820). He was also a Justice of the Peace from 1779. He was involved in the slave trade and he is listed amongst 'the Company of Merchants trading to Africa' in 1807.

83 (not illus.)
Goblet
Glass painted in enamel colours with Royal Coat of Arms and on the reverse a depiction of a three-masted ship and the inscription 'Success to the African trade of WHITE-HAVEN' and signed 'Beilby juvt invt & pinxt', by William Beilby (1740-1819), Newcastle upon Tyne, c.1762-63
250mm high
Whitehaven Museum

This is one of a small number of goblets bearing the Royal coat of arms produced by William Beilby using the technique he discovered in 1761 to fuse enamel on to glass. The other surviving goblets all feature the

Prince of Wales's device on the reverse. This goblet was almost certainly produced to commemorate the vessel KING GEORGE which was built in Whitehaven in 1762-63 for the slave trade. John Paul Jones, 'the founder of the American Navy', was third mate on the maiden voyage.

84 (illus. p. 37)
GRAND TURK
Exhibition model by W. G. Leavitt, of Salem, Massachussets
Scale 1:48
NMGM (Merseyside Maritime Museum). 1952.1

This brig of about 300 tons was built at Wiscasset, Maine, in the USA in 1812 and was purchased by a group of merchants from Salem who gave her the name GRAND TURK. She was used in privateering, particularly against the British, with whom the Americans were at war from 1812 to 1818. Although pierced for 18 guns, the model only shows 16. The vessel is typical of the fine lined vessels which were used in slave trading.

85 (illus. p. 39)
WATT
Contemporary builders' model, 1797
Scale 1:24
Williamson Art Gallery & Museum, Birkenhead. 82.186

The WATT, built by Edward Grayson of Liverpool for the firm of Watt & Walker, was launched in February 1797. She was a 22-gun ship-rigged vessel of 564 tons. The firm's main business was in trade with Jamaica, where the Watt family also had an estate, and the vessel was mainly employed bringing back sugar from Jamaica.

86 (illus. p. 38)
Ship bowl, 'Success To The Dobson 1770'
Depiction of ship painted in under-glazed blue, enamelled in red and green, tin-glazed earthenware, Liverpool, 1770
270 (dia) × 110mm
NMGM (Liverpool Museum). 50.60.13

The DOBSON was a 200-ton ship built in Liverpool in 1770. Her principal sharcholder was William Davenport,

one of the most active slave traders in the port, who invested in some 120 slave voyages during a career of nearly 40 years.

87 (illus. p. 41)
A Liverpool slave ship
About 1780, by William Jackson, (active about 1780-1803), oil on canvas, signed 'W.Jackson Pnx'
1040 × 1090mm
NMGM (Merseyside Maritime Museum). 1964.227.2

This unidentified 16-gun ship is typical of the vessels used in the slave trade. She is shown in a port profile against a wooded coastline, intended to represent West Africa. The ship is about to drop anchor and a boat is to be launched. The ventilation holes below her gun deck suggest she is intended to carry slaves. Recent cleaning has revealed three small boats with Africans on board approaching from the coast.

88 (col. illus. p. 72)
Armed brig in the Mersey
About 1810, by John Jenkinson (active 1790-1821), oil on canvas, signed 'J. Jenkinson'
810 × 1120mm
NMGM (Merseyside Maritime Museum). 1991.5

Although this 14-gun brig is unidentified, she is typical of the large merchant vessels which were involved in slaving from Liverpool. The Liverpool Guide of 1796 comments, 'The Guineamen [slave traders] here, are in general the handsomest ships; being every way modelled after the Frigates, and rather more ornamented'. The ship is shown in a starboard view in the Mersey off the Wirral coast, near Birkenhead.

81

The Middle Passage

The Middle Passage was a dehumanising experience, characterized by fear and brutality. Male Africans were shackled below deck and men, women and children were subject to punishment and abuse from the crew.

89

89
Shackles, neck iron and chains
Wrought iron, 18th century
NMGM (Merseyside Maritime Museum).
N/N

90
Shackles, leg irons
Wrought iron, 18th century
295mm
NMGM (Liverpool Museum). 1956.26.709

91
Shackles, leg irons
Wrought iron, 18th century
400mm
NMGM (Liverpool Museum). 56.24.135

92 (illus. p. 34)
Cat-o'-nine-tails
Nine knotted cords, with wooden handle covered with green and red baize, late 19th century
1143mm
National Maritime Museum, London

Although this is an example of a later Royal Naval cat-o'nine tails, it is identical to the sort used on board vessels during the slaving period.

90

93 (illus. p. 46)
Grape shot in bag
Lead, 18th century
NMGM (Merseyside Maritime Museum).
1986.201.84B

94 (illus. p. 103)
Flintlock blunderbuss
English, late 18th century
810mm
NMGM (Merseyside Maritime Museum).
60.86.1

This is the sort of weapon that was used on board ship to intimidate and quell rebellions.

91

95 (not illus.)
Chart of the Atlantic, with a voyage of a slave ship
1794
540 × 1410mm
NMGM (Merseyside Maritime Museum). OA 1866

96 (illus. p. 47)
Log book of the UNITY
1769-71
210 × 175mm
NMGM (Merseyside Maritime Museum). 1993.108

This log covers a slaving voyage of the UNITY from Liverpool to Cape Coast Castle and Jamaica, returning to Liverpool in May 1771. She was owned by the Earle family, who were important merchants in Liverpool in the 18th and 19th centuries. Although they traded to the Mediterranean and elsewhere much of their business involved the slave trade and planta-tion goods from the West Indies.

97 (illus. p. 46)
Necklace of nine charm pendants
Cloth, leather and horn, Mande, Gambia
640 mm
NMGM (Liverpool Museum). 13.2.69.7

98 (illus. p. 34)
Surgical instrument set, cased, by Whitford
London, late 18th/early 19th century
455 × 222mm
Science Museum, London. A600582

Surgeons were carried on many slave ships, though their abilities varied greatly. Most of their work involved examining captives and dealing with disease. They would rarely have had recourse to their instruments.

Destinations

The majority of enslaved Africans were taken to the Caribbean, where England, France and the other Euro-pean participants all had colonies by the end of the 17th century. Equally large numbers were also taken to Brazil, particularly in the 19th century. Spanish colonies in Central and South America were an important destina-tion in the early years of slavery. Only about 1 in 20 Africans were taken directly to the Southern states of North America.

99
'A / GENERAL CHART / OF / THE WEST INDIA ISLANDS / WITH THE ADJACENT COASTS OF / THE SPANISH CONTINENT,/ BY L.S. DE LA ROCHETTE, / M.DCCXCVI. / LONDON./ PUBLISHED BY W. FADEN GEOGRAPHER TO THE KING / AND TO H.R.H. THE PRINCE OF WALES,/ SEPTEMBER 22D 1796', printed coloured chart
1796
623 × 880mm
NMGM (Merseyside Maritime Museum). 1992.141

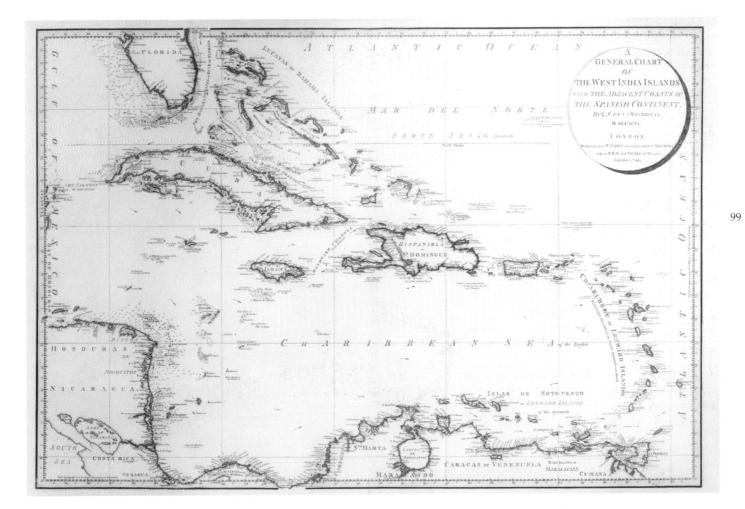

99

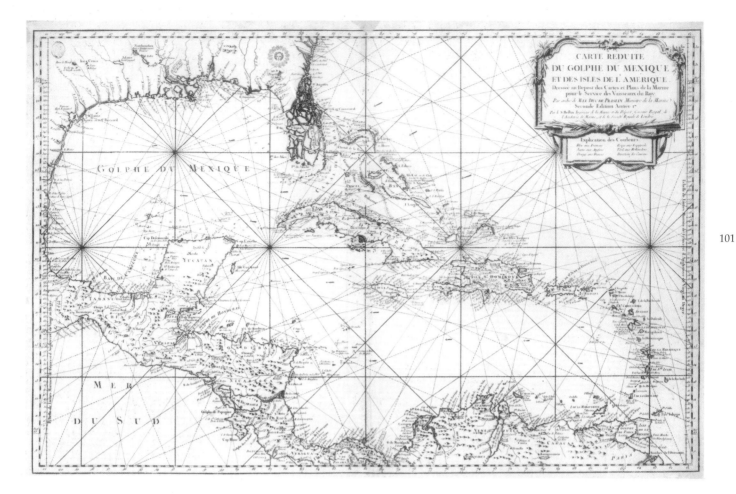

100 (illus. p. 18)
Chart of Caribbean and Gulf of
Mexico, printed coloured chart,
'Insulae / Americanae / in Oceano
Septemtrionali ac / Regiones
Adiacentes / ac de May usque ad
Lineam equinoctialem / Par
Nicolaum Visscher / Cum Privilegio
Ordinum Hollandaise et Westfrisiae'
Nicolas Visscher, Amsterdam, c.1700
540 × 435mm
National Maritime Museum, London.
G245 1/8

101
Map of Caribbean and Gulf of
Mexico, printed chart, 'Carte Reduite
/ du GOLPHE DU MEXIQUE / et des
INDES DE L'AMERIQUE .... Seconde
edition   Année 17 ... Par le S. Bellin'
Jacques Nicolas Bellin, Paris, 1770
805 × 535mm
National Maritime Museum, London.
G245 1/14

102
Map of Caribbean, printed chart,
inscribed 'Pascaerte vande /
CARIBES /....'
Johannes Van Keulen, Amsterdam, 1st half
18th century
580 × 510mm
National Maritime Museum, London.
245 2/2

103 (illus. p. 56)
Plan of Havana, with inset map of
Cuba, printed, 'An exact plan of the /
City, Fortifications & Harbour of /
Havana / in the Island of Cuba /
From an original Drawing taken on
the Spot / Universal Magazine, J.
Hinton, Newgate Street.'
John Hinton, from the Universal Maga-
zine, London, c.1762
340 × 255mm
National Maritime Museum, London.
G245 6/10

104 (illus. p. 50)
Map of St Domingue, printed chart,
'Carte de L'ISLE DE SAINT

DOMINIQUE ... Par le Sr. Bellin ...
1764'
Jacques Nicolas Bellin, Paris, 1764
905 × 570mm
National Maritime Museum, London.
245 8/13

105 (illus. p. 50)
Map of Jamaica divided into parishes,
printed chart, 'DESCRIPTIO per
JOHANNEM OGILIUM
Cosmographum Regium 1761'
John Ogilby, London, 1671
520 × 415mm
National Maritime Museum, London.
245 11/3

106 (illus. p. 18)
Map of the Virgin Islands, printed
coloured chart, 'THE VIRGIN IS-
LANDS / from / ENGLISH and
DANISH SURVEYS / BY / THOMAS
JEFFERYS / Geographer to the King'
Thomas Jefferys, printed and published by
Robert Sayer, London, 1775
590 × 442mm
National Maritime Museum, London.
G245 14/7

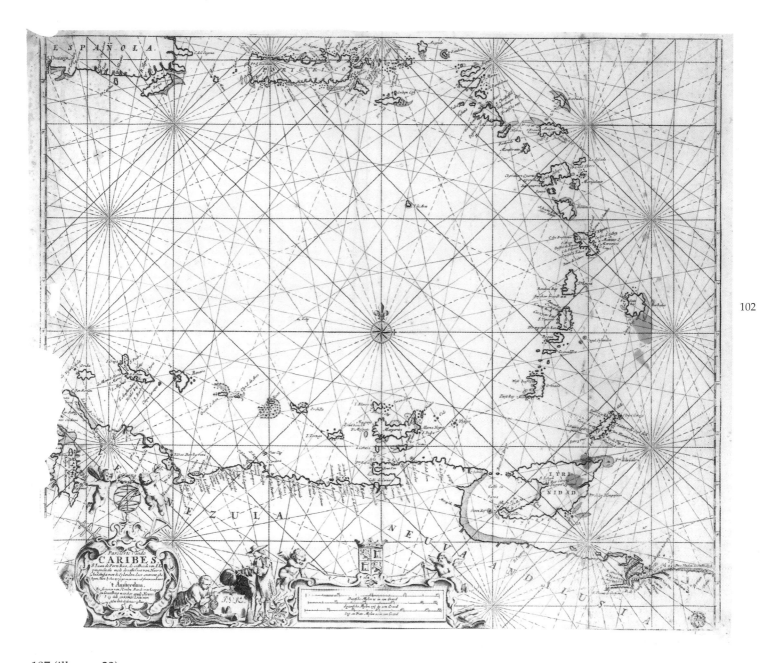

107 (illus. p. 23)
Map of Curacao, printed chart with plan, elevation and six views, 'Nieuwe Afteekening / van het Eyland / Curacao / verto2onende alle deselfe geleegentheedom / mitsgaders de haven van / St. Anna en 't Fort Amsterdam / Int grood als ook hoe sig dit Eyland / uyt der zee vertoont / Tot Amsterdam by / Gerard van Keulen'

Gerard van Keulen, Amsterdam, 1st quarter 18th century
590 × 390mm
National Maritime Museum, London.
G245 15/14

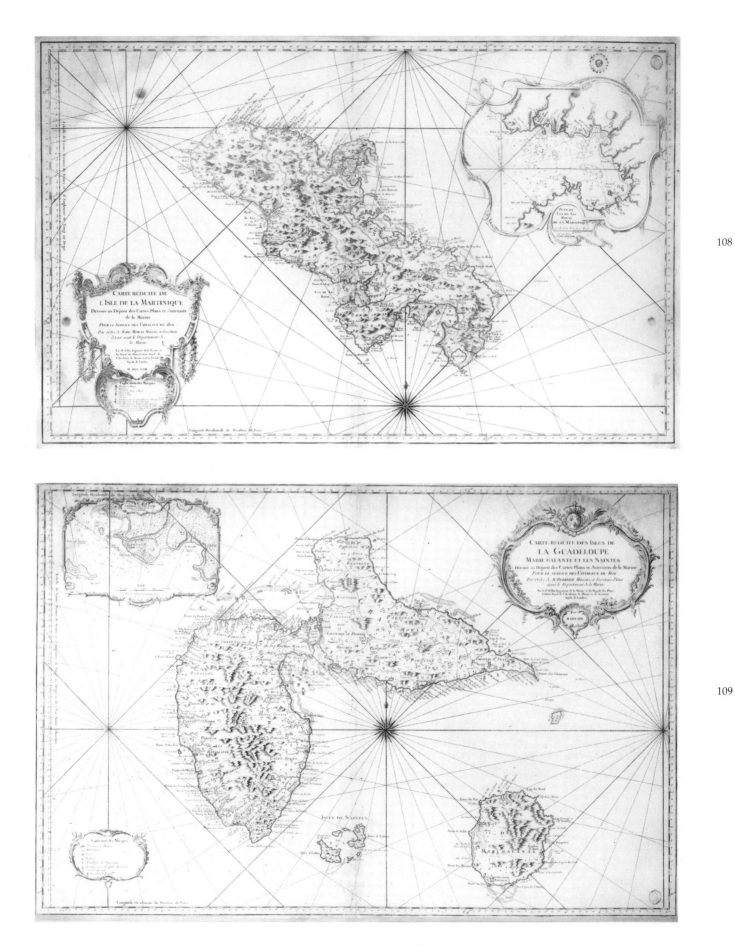

108

109

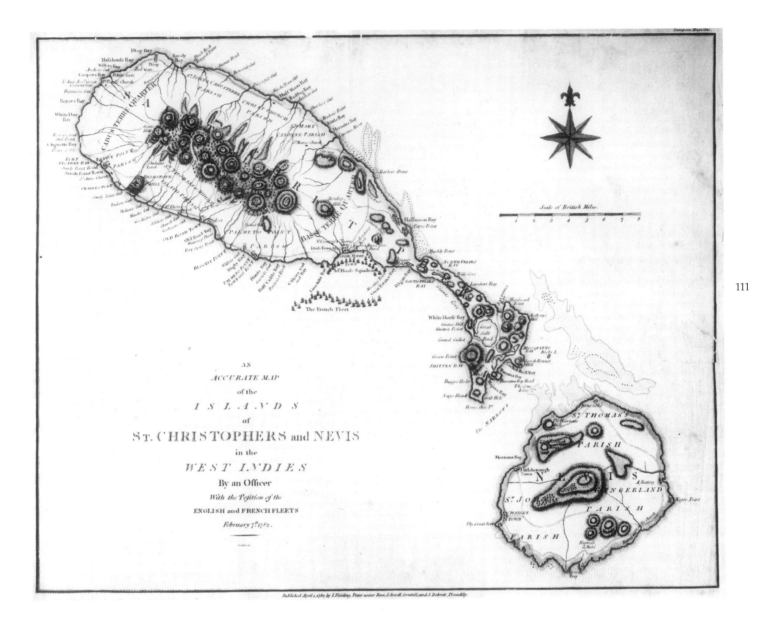

108

Map of Martinique, printed chart with inset of harbour of Cul de Sac Marin, 'Carte Reduit de / L'ISLE DE MARTIN IQUE ... Par M. Bellin ... 1758'

Jacques Nicolas Bellin, Paris, 1758
880 × 560mm
National Maritime Museum, London.
245 15/33

109

Map of Guadeloupe, printed chart, 'Carte Reduit des ISLES DE / LA GUADELOUPE / MARIE GALANTE ET LES SAINTES ... Par le Sr. Bellin ... 1759'

Jacques Nicolas Bellin, Paris, 1759
870 × 580mm
National Maritime Museum, London.
245 15/34

110 (illus. p. 23)

Map of St Lucia, printed chart with insets of Carenage, Cul de Sac des Roseaux and Grand Islet et du choc, 'Carte de / L'ISLE DE SAINTE LUCIE / Par le Sr. Bellin ... 1763'

Jacques Nicolas Bellin, Paris, 1763
880 × 560mm
National Maritime Museum, London.
G245 15/35

111

Coloured facsimile map of St Kitts and Nevis, 'An Accurate Map of the Islands of St Christophers and Nevis in the West Indies, By an Officer, With the Position of the English and French fleets, February 7th 1782 / Published April 1, 1782, by I. Fielding, Paternoster Row; J. Sewell, Cornhill; and J. Debrett, Picadilly'

London, 1782
310 × 375mm
National Maritime Museum, London.
G345 15/3

112 (illus. p. 148)

24 Shilling Piece, obverse: crowned double monogram of Frederic V 'D G DAN NOR VAN GOT REX', reverse: image of ship, 'XXIIII SKILL DANSKE AMERICANSK M 1764'

Silver, Danish West Indies, 1764
NMGM (Liverpool Museum). 15.2.89.290

113 (illus. p. 55)
24 Shilling Piece, obverse: monogram of Christian VII 'D G DAN NOR VAN GOT REX', reverse: image of ship, 'XXIIII SKILL DANSKE AMERICANSK M 1767'
Silver, Danish West Indies, 1767
NMGM (Liverpool Museum). 15.2.89.91

114
12 Shilling Piece, obverse: monogram of Christian VII 'D G DAN NOR VAN GOT REX', reverse: image of ship, 'XII SKILL DANSKE AMERICANSK M 1767'
Silver, Danish West Indies, 1767
NMGM (Liverpool Museum). 15.2.89.292

115
12 Shilling Piece, obverse: monogram of Christian VII 'D G DAN NOR VAN GOT REX', reverse: image of ship, 'XII SKILL DANSKE AMERICANSK M 1767'
Danish West Indies, 1767
NMGM (Liverpool Museum). 15.2.89.293

116 (illus. p. 52)
One Penny Token, obverse: image of a head 'I SERVE', reverse: image of a pineapple, 'BARBADOES PENNY 1788'
Copper, Barbados, 1788
NMGM (Liverpool Museum). N/N

117
One Penny token, obverse: image of a head 'I SERVE', reverse: image of a pineapple, 'BARBADOES PENNY 1788'
Copper, Barbados, 1788
NMGM (Liverpool Museum). 1966.300.196

118
One Penny token, obverse: image of a head 'I SERVE', reverse: image of Neptune, 'BARBADOES PENNY 1792'
Copper, Barbados, 1792
NMGM (Liverpool Museum). N/N

119
Half-penny token, obverse: image of a head 'I SERVE', reverse: image of a pineapple, 'BARBADOES HALF-PENNY 1788'
Copper, Barbados, 1788
NMGM (Liverpool Museum). N/N

112

115

114

117

119

These tokens are the earliest minted coins from Barbados, probably struck by order of Sir Philip Gibbs, a plantation owner. They were designed by John Milton but were never recognised as legal colonial coinage.

120
One Stiver, Demarary & Essequebo, obverse: bust of king, 'GEORGIUS III D.G. REX', reverse: crown and oak leaves, 'COLONIES OF ESSEQUEBO AND DEMERARY TOKEN 1813 ONE STIVER'
Copper, 1813
NMGM (Liverpool Museum). N/N

118

120

123

121

121
Section of coin, stamped with emblem
Silver, Curacao, Dutch West Indies,
1807-15
NMGM (Liverpool Museum). N/N

122
Section of coin, stamped with emblem
Curacao, Dutch West Indies, 1807-15
NMGM (Liverpool Museum). N/N

123
Cut silver, stamped with emblem
St Lucia
NMGM (Liverpool Museum). 1966.300.194

124 (col. illus. p.1)
Seal, Royal coat of arms of George III,
'OFFICE FOR REGISTRATION OF
SLAVES DEMERARY'
Wax, Demerara
274 × 205mm
NMGM (Merseyside Maritime Museum).
51.111

125 (illus. p. 52)
Auction hammer
Ivory with silver band, (?) 19th century
32mm(dia) × 125mm
Whitby Museum

Slave Life in the Americas.

There are relatively few objects
directly associated with the lives of
slaves. Many of these are instruments
of torture or punishment. Slaves
themselves had few possessions. In
maroon communities craftsmen
produced a wider range of items that

122

were necessary to sustain everyday
life. Music and dance played an
important part and the continuity of
an African tradition can be seen in a
small selection of instruments.

126
'The TOBACCO MANUFACTORY in
different branches, Engrav'd for the
Universal Magazine 1750 for J.Hinton
at the Kings Arms in St Pauls Church
Yard London'
Engraving, laid off-white paper and black
ink
203 × 245mm
NMGM (Merseyside Maritime Museum).
1994.21

Tobacco was labour intensive crop but
which also required skilled handling,
particularly in the drying and finish-
ing processes depicted here. Tobacco
was mainly grown in North America,
especially in Virginia and Maryland,
but was also cultivated in Brazil.

127
Stool with snake motif
Carved wood, Saramaccer tribe, Ganya
Condree Valley, Upper Surinam River,
Dutch Guyana
241 × 311 × 330mm
American Museum of Natural History,
New York. 26.203

128
Grinding board, for mashing peanuts
Carved wood, Aucaner tribe, Moompusu
Village, Tapanahoni River, Dutch Guyana
140 × 489 × 349mm
American Museum of Natural History,
New York. 26.588

129
Comb with bird motif
Wood, Aucaner tribe, Lassa Bakka river,
Sara Creek District, Dutch Guiana
343 × 410 × 13mm
American Museum of Natural History,
New York. 26.414

Wood carving is an important feature
of the maroon communities of Dutch
Guyana and a wide range of objects
were produced. Whilst many items
are similar to those found in Africa,
decorative wood-carving only began
in the early 19th century and its
development was not derived from
African traditions or styles.

126

The TOBACCO-MANUFACTORY in different Branches.

Engraved for the Universal-Magazine 1750 for J. Hinton at the Kings Arms in S.t Pauls Church Yard London.

129

127

128

130

130
Bread bowl
Carved wood, mid-19th century
480 × 310 × 115mm
Texas Memorial Museum. 1966.1

131
Rolling pin
Carved wood, mid-19th century
50(dia) × 350mm
Texas Memorial Museum. 1966.2

These two kitchen items are reputed to have been made by slaves.

132 (illus. p. 110)
Drum
Wood, cedar root and deer skin, Virginia, late 17th century
290(dia) × 410mm
Museum of Mankind, London. SL1368

This Asante-style drum was acquired by Sir Hans Sloane (1660-1753) in Virginia. As a physician and naturalist he travelled widely in the American colonies. The drum is an example of how cultural traditions were transferred from Africa to the Americas.

133 (illus. p. 47)
Drum, 'The Nanda'
Paramacca tribe, Seeton Ponta Village, Marowyne River, French Guyana
267 × 438(dia)mm
American Museum of Natural History, New York. 26.544

134 (illus. p. 110)
Marimbola, with red, black and white painting
Wood, Loiza Aldea, Puerto Rico, 1950
445 × 595 × 173mm
Museo Universidad de Puerto Rico

135
Drum, with red, black and yellow painting
Wood with rope and leather, Loiza Aldea, Puerto Rico, 1950
432(dia) × 445mm
Museo Universidad de Puerto Rico

These instruments demonstrate that the continuity of African traditions amongst slave and former slave communities has lasted through until the present day.

135

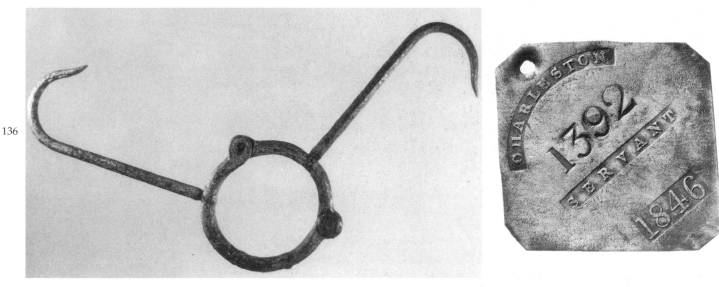

136

139

136
Neck shackle
Wrought iron, 19th century
560 × 343mm
Museo Universidad de Puerto Rico

137
Poster advertising for a runaway
slave
St Louis, 23 August 1852
290 × 460mm
Hull Museums. 24/52

138 (illus. p. 115)
Punishment collar
Wrought iron, 18th century
188 × 310mm
Manchester Museum. 0.9322/289

139
Slave badge, stamped
'CHARLESTON / 1392 / SERVANT /
1846'
Copper alloy, 1846
American Numismatic Society, New York.
0000.999.37277

In the early 19th century, slaves in
Charleston, South Carolina, were
required to register their names and
occupations and wear an identity
badge. In 1848 this requirement was
also extended to free black people.

137

$2,500 REWARD!

**RANAWAY, from the Subscriber, resi-
ding in Mississippi county, Mo., on Monday the 5th inst., my
Negro Man named GEORGE.**

Said negro is five feet ten inches high, of dark complexion, he
plays well on the Violin and several other instruments. He is
a shrewd, smart fellow and of a very affable countenance, and
is twenty-five years of age. If said negro is taken and confined in St. Louis Jail, or brought to this county so that I get
him, the above reward of $1,000 will be promptly paid.

JOHN MEANS.

Also, from Radford E. Stanley,

A NEGRO MAN SLAVE, NAMED NOAH,

Full 6 feet high; black complexion; full eyes; free spoken
and intelligent; will weigh about 180 pounds; 32 years old;
had with him 2 or 3 suits of clothes, white hat, short blue blanket coat, a pair of saddle bags, a pocket compass, and supposed
to have $350 or $400 with him.

ALSO--- A NEGRO MAN NAMED HAMP,

Of dark copper color, big thick lips, about 6 feet high, weighs about 175
pounds, 36 years old, with a scar in the forehead from the kick of a horse; had
a lump on one of his wrists and is left-handed. Had with him two suits of clothes,
one a casinet or cloth coat and grey pants.

Also, Negro Man Slave named BOB,

Copper color, high cheek bones, 5 feet 11 inches high, weighs about 150 pounds,
22 years old, very white teeth and a space between the centre of the upper teeth
Had a blue blanket sack coat with red striped linsey lining. Supposed to have
two suits of clothes with him; is a little lame in one ancle.
$1,000 will be given for George----$600 for Noah---$450 for Hamp---$450
for Bob; if caught in a free State, or a reasonable compensation if caught in
a Slave State, if delivered to the Subscribers in Miss. Co., Mo., or confined in
Jail in St. Louis, so that we get them   Refer to

**JOHN MEANS &
R. E. STANLEY.**

ST. LOUIS, August 23, 1852.   (PLEASE STICK UP.)

140

only the name and offence but the time, place, extent of the punishment and by whom authorised and inflicted.

143 (illus. p. 65)
Receipt from Court of Baltimore to Mr R. O'Ferrale for payment of $1000 for female slaves
Baltimore, 5 September 1859
Hull Museums. Box 10/15

European Rewards

A range of raw materials was imported into Europe which were directly produced by slave labour or were paid for from the profits of the slavery. Wealthy Europeans in the 18th and early 19th centuries were surrounded with reminders of transatlantic slavery whether by the sugar on their tables or the mahogany chairs they sat on. The huge scale of production also brought many items, like sugar, within reach of the poor.

144 (not illus.)
'Plan of the City of Bristol and its Suburbs', showing sugar refineries
Commenced 1813 by John Plumley and completed 1828 by George C. Ashmead
Bristol Museums & Art Galleries. M766

140
Shackles
Wrought iron
Chicago Historical Society

141 (illus. p. 67)
Letter to Thomas Eaton, Swansea, from his slave, Pheba
Kingston, Jamaica, 12 March 1793
305 × 186mm
Hull Museums. Box 7/18

Pheba writes to complain about ill treatment she and her daughter have suffered when hired out.

142 (illus. p. 49)
Punishment Records, Friendship Plantation
Jamaica, January-June 1828
355 × 475mm
Hull Museums. 46.72

Records of punishments were kept on many plantations. They listed not

145 (only one illus.)
Two sugar loaves
515 × 130(dia)mm; 270 × 120(dia)mm
Tate & Lyle, London

146
Sugar breaker, 'SYMES PATENT / LONDON'
Cast iron, 19th century
380 × 640mm
Tate & Lyle, London

147
Sugar bowl
China, white ground with gilt decoration, c.1800
113(dia) × 117mm
NMGM (Liverpool Museum). 55.20.16

148
Sugar nippers
Late 18th/early 19th century
262mm
NMGM (Liverpool Museum). 1969.216.7

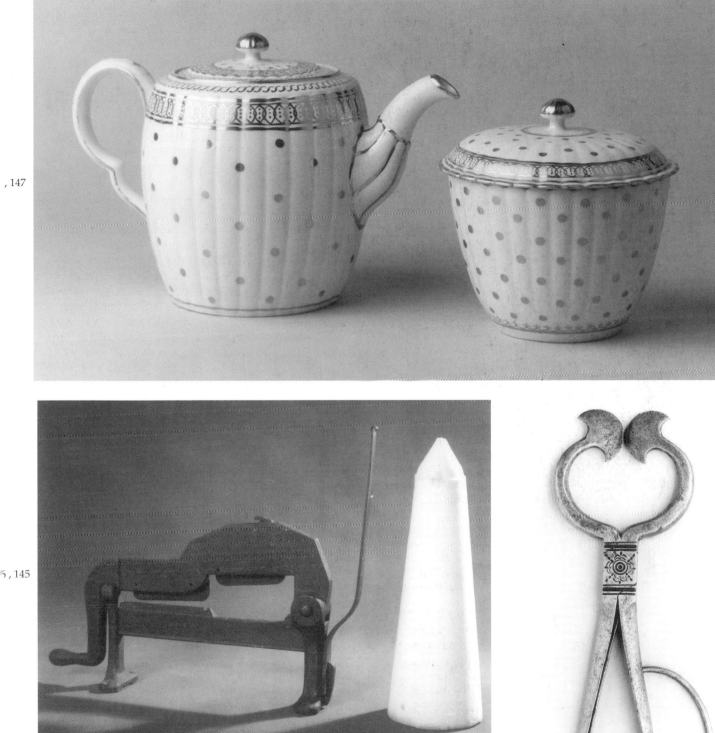

, 147

6 , 145

148

155

150

149
Tea pot
China, white ground with gilt decoration, c.1800
139 × 80mm
NMGM (Liverpool Museum). 55.20.14

150
Coffee pot, with scene of couple seated in garden being served by a black servant
Creamware, transfer-printed in black, Liverpool, c.1760-65
109(dia) × 215mm
NMGM (Liverpool Museum). 1980.24.2

151
Coffee cup, with scene of couple seated in garden being served by a black servant
Creamware, transfer-printed in black, Liverpool, c.1760-65
38(dia) × 62mm
NMGM (Liverpool Museum). 59.119.107

Sugar was the most important of the raw materials brought back to Europe, where it was refined and sold. It was used to sweeten the naturally bitter beverages, like coffee and tea, and made them hugely popular. As one early 19th century dictionary put it, sugar was "one of the indispensable necessaries of life".

152 (col. illus. p. 72)
Punch pot, 'IAM + GIBLET / 1766'
Earthenware, black ground hand painted with gilt decoration, 1766
NMGM (Liverpool Museum) M1240–1

153
Pepper pots
Pewter, late 18th century
63(dia) × 109mm
NMGM (Liverpool Museum). N/N

Although most pepper came from the East, it was also grown in the Americas and regularly figures as a cargo on ships returning to Europe.

151

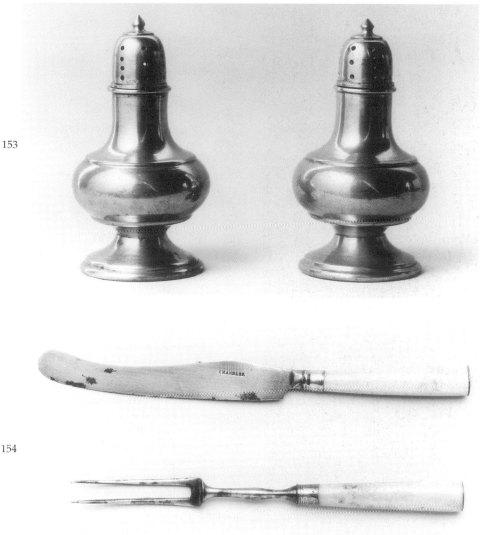

153

154

155

154
Knife and fork, knife blade stamped 'CHANDLER'
Ivory handles, late 18th century
276mm; 252mm
NMGM (Liverpool Museum). N/N

Ivory was widely used as handles for cutlery from the 17th century and although much of it came from the Indian sub-continent, Africa remained an important source.

155
Bottle containing ginger powder, with printed label 'PREPARED POWDER / OF / JAMAICAN GINGER'
66(dia) × 205mm
NMGM (Merseyside Maritime Museum).
1986.201.7c

Ginger was an important spice which was grown on many Caribbean islands and was regularly used by European cooks. This sample, probably dating from the early 19th century, was part of a collection of items preserved by the Wynn family of North Wales.

156 (not illus.)
Chair
Mahogany, English, c.1730-40
971mm high
NMGM (Lady Lever Art Gallery). LL4346

157 (not illus.)
Bracket clock
Satinwood, 18th century
281 × 164 × 421mm
NMGM (Lady Lever Art Gallery.). LL4461

158 (not illus.)
Knife box
Mahogany, English, early 19th century
204 × 222 × 309mm
NMGM (Lady Lever Art Gallery). LL4793

159
Wood samples
9 samples of cedar, brasiletto, fustic, logwood, camphor, lignum vitae, satinwood, pimento wood and mahogany
56 × 30mm
NMGM (Liverpool Museum). 1986.149

When mahogany was introduced into Britain in the early 18th century, it was known as Jamaica wood because the island was then the principal source. It became the most popular wood for furniture making and was also used for doors, panelling and other interior details into the 19th century. Supplies were obtained from many parts of Central and South America, including Honduras and Cuba. Other American woods, such as satinwood, were used as inlay and decoration.

160
Dye recipe book
1821
Museum of Science & Industry, Manchester

Other timbers, such as logwood and fustic, were imported from the Caribbean and Central America. They were used as dyes in the textile industry and as stains in furniture making.

Black People in Europe

Although the number of Africans in Europe was small in relation to the

159

millions who were transported to the Americas, there was a significant Black presence in all Western European countries. They are, however, only rarely represented in contemporary paintings and illustrations

161 (illus p. 84)
Olaudah Equiano
British School, oil on canvas, late 18th century
618 × 515mm
Royal Albert Memorial Museum, Exeter. 19.1943

162
'The Interesting Narrative of the life of Olaudah Equiano, or Gustavus Vassa, the African. Written by himself', 6th edition
London, 1793
173 × 113mm
Private collection, UK

Olaudah Equiano (about 1743-1797) is one of the few Africans whose personal story and experience of being enslaved has come down to us, through his autobiography, published in 1789. After his escape from slavery, he settled in London and was an active campaigner against the slave trade. He toured throughout Britain speaking against slavery. The frontispiece reproduces the only known representation of the man who was perhaps the best known African in Britain in the 18th century.

163 (illus. p. 85)
The Black Boy
William Windus (1822-1907), oil on canvas
761 × 635mm
NMGM (Walker Art Gallery). 1601

This young African boy is said to have come to Liverpool as a stowaway and was engaged by Windus as an errand boy. It is reputed to have been painted in 1844 and thus the boy probably came to Liverpool on a vessel carrying palm oil. There were other Africans in the port at this time, mainly as a result of the trade with West Africa and the employment of Africans as crew.

160

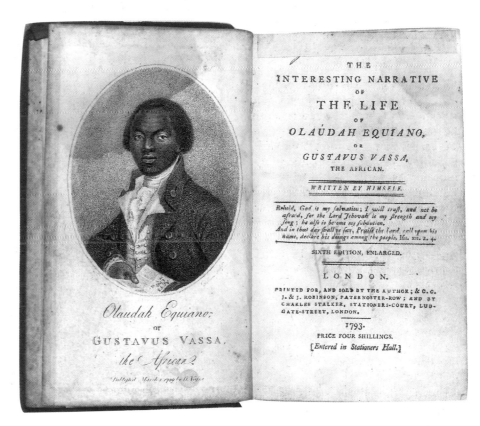

162

164
Tile 'The Turkish Merchant'
Tin-glazed earthenware transfer-printed in black, Liverpool
126 x 126mm
NMGM (Liverpool Museum). 15.12.20.16

164

166

Abolition and Emancipation

The campaigns for the abolition of the slave trade and the emancipation from slavery were popular subjects for the producers of commemorative china and of tokens and medals.

165 (illus. p. 48)
Figure of an enslaved African breaking free of his chains
Carved wood, American, late 19th century
1900mm high
NMGM (Merseyside Maritime Museum).
1993.170

This full-sized figure is similar to other carved figures in the American folk art tradition. An enslaved African is represented in the act of breaking free of his chains in what may be seen as a symbolic gesture.

166
Epistles from the yearly meeting of Friends, 16??-1817
Published London, 1818
230 × 150mm
NMGM (Merseyside Maritime Museum).
1993.231

167 (illus. p. 91)
William Roscoe
After John Williamson (1751-1818), oil on canvas, 428 × 360mm (painted surface within oval)
NMGM (Walker Art Gallery). 6136

William Roscoe (1753-1831) is probably the best known of the supporters of abolition in Liverpool. A self made man, he began his career as a lawyer and later moved into banking. He had wide literary and artistic interests and was a noted writer and collector. He wrote a long poem, 'The Wrongs of Africa', and many pamphlets in favour of abolition. Opinion in Liverpool was generally pro-slavery and like other abolitionists, Roscoe tended to work behind the scenes rather than openly declaring his views. He was the town's Member of Parliament in 1806-07 but this was not an issue in his election and he was not active in the debates which lead to abolition.

168 (illus. p. 91)
Patch box, with abolitionist motif, 'AM I NOT A MAN AND A BROTHER'
Enamel on copper, South Staffordshire, c.1790
48 × 39 × 26mm
NMGM (Liverpool Museum). 1987.212.3

169 (illus. p. 90)
'African Hospitality', illustrating the verse 'Dauntless they plunge amidst the vengeful waves,/ And snatch from death the lovely sinking fair– / Their friendly efforts lo! each Briton saves / Perhaps their future Tyrants now they spare'
Engraved by J R Smith, King Street, Covent Garden, London, after George Morland, 1 February 1791
640 × 803mm
NMGM (Merseyside Maritime Museum).
1991.389.1

170 (illus. p. 90)
'Slave Trade', illustrating the verse 'Lo! the poor Captive with distraction wild / Views his dear Partner torn from his embrace!/ A different Captain buys his Wife and Child. / What time can from his Soul such ills erase'
Engraved by J R Smith, King Street, Covent Garden, London, after George Morland, 1 February 1791
640 × 803mm
NMGM (Merseyside Maritime Museum).
1991.389.2

171 (illus. p. 91)
One Penny token, obverse: chained slave kneeling in supplication, 'AM I NOT A MAN AND A BROTHER', reverse: WHATSOEVER / YE WOULD THAT / MEN SHOULD DO / UNTO YOU, DO YE / EVEN SO TO / THEM'
c.1790
NMGM (Liverpool Museum). DH 235

172
Half-penny token, obverse: chained slave kneeling in supplication, 'AM I NOT A MAN AND A BROTHER', reverse: clasped hands, 'MAY SLAVERY & OPPRESSION CEASE THROUGHOUT THE WORLD'
NMGM (Liverpool Museum). 68.219.151

172

173 (illus. p. 87)
Half-penny token, obverse: 'AM I NOT A MAN AND A BROTHER', reverse: clasped hands, 'MAY SLAVERY & OPPRESSION CEASE THROUGHOUT THE WORLD'
NMGM (Liverpool Museum). 69.109.411

174
Half-penny token, obverse:'AM I NOT A MAN AND A BROTHER', reverse: 'WHATSOEVER YE WOULD THAT MEN SHOULD DO TO YOU, DO YE EVEN SO TO THEM'
NMGM (Liverpool Museum). N/N

These tokens were produced for The Society for the Suppression of the African Slave Trade, which was founded in 1787. They were issued between 1787 and the abolition of the trade in 1807.

175 (not illus.)
One Cent, Sierra Leone Company, 1791, obverse: Lion, 'SIERRA LEONE COMPANY, AFRICA', reverse: clasped hands, 'ONE CENT PIECE 1791'
Bronze, 1791
NMGM (Liverpool Museum). 66.300.193

176
One Cent, Sierra Leone Company, 1791, Obverse: Lion,'Sierra Leone Company, Africa', Reverse: clasped hands, 'One Cent Piece 1791'
NMGM (Liverpool Museum). N/N

These coins were designed by Matthew Boulton and struck at his Soho Mint in Birmingham. They were produced for the Sierra Leone Company, which was responsible for the establishment of a colony of ex-slaves, who had fought for the British during the American War of Independence but who were not welcome in England.

177 (col. illus. p. 71)
Oval épergne, by Pitts and Preedy, engraved with the arms of the Town of Liverpool and those of Machell of Penny Bridge, Co. Lancaster, impaling Penny, inscribed 'This is one of two Pieces of Silver Plate presented to JAMES PENNY ESQr by The COR-

174

176

PORATION OF LIVERPOOL 1792.' A later inscription on the central bowl reads 'John Penny Machell Esquire, of Penny Bridge and Hollow Oak gave on 23rd October 1877 to Andrew Hay Wilson this piece of plate which was originally presented to their Grandfather James Penny by the Corporation of Liverpool.'
Silver plate, 1792
457mm high, 114oz
NMGM (Liverpool Museum). 1973.278

This épergne was one of two pieces of plate, valued at £100, which were presented to James Penny in 1792 by the Liverpool Town Council in recognition of his support for the slave trade. He was a prominent Liverpool slave trader and regularly sent vessels to the West African coast and Angola. Penny gave evidence in the parliamentary enquiries into the trade and, with others, had been given the freedom of the borough in 1788 'for the very essential advantages derived to the trade of Liverpool from their evidence in support of the African slave trade, and for the public spirit they have manifested'.

178 (illus. p. 45)
25 centimes, obverse: palm tree and trophy of arms and flags, reverse: '25c' in snake 'REPUBLIQUE D'HAYTI AN 13'
Silver, Haiti, Petion Republic, 1816
NMGM (Liverpool Museum) 75.65.91

Haiti, the former French colony of St Domingue, was the first Caribbean island to achieve independence in 1804 after a long and bloody revolt which began in 1789. A separate republic under Alexander Petion was declared in the south-west of the island in 1807.

179
Copy of information relating to an inquiry into the treatment of a female slave by Rev. Mr Bridges, Rector of St Ann's, Jamaica
Jamaica, 10 March 1831
350 × 215mm
NMGM (Merseyside Maritime Museum) 1993.129

5446
537 HZ

JAMAICA.

RETURN to an Address to His late MAJESTY, dated 12 May 1830;—*for,*

COPY of any Information which may have been received from *Jamaica,* respecting an INQUIRY into the TREATMENT of a FEMALE SLAVE, by the Reverend Mr. *Bridges,* Rector of *St. Ann's,* in that Island; with the MINUTES of EVIDENCE taken by the MAGISTRATES on that occasion, and the result of the Inquiry.

Colonial Department,
Downing-street,
February 1831.

HOWICK.

Ordered, by The House of Commons, *to be Printed,*
10 *March* 1831.

231.

179

180 (illus. p. 93)
Plate with abolitionist motifs and mottoes
White china, printed in brown, early 19th century
225(dia)mm
NMGM (Liverpool Museum). 54.124.5

181 (illus. p. 93)
Comport with abolitionist motifs and mottoes
White china, printed in brown, early 19th century
335 × 280 × 162mm
NMGM (Liverpool Museum). 54.124.1

182 (illus. p. 93)
Small cup with tropical scene and overseer whipping a kneeling and chained slave, 'From Sun to Sun the Negro toils / No smiles reward his trusty care, / And when the indignant mind recoils, / His doom is whips and black despair'
White china, printed in green, 19th century
75(dia) × 68mm
NMGM (Liverpool Museum). 54.171.486

183 (illus. p. 94)
Sugar bowl inscribed in gilt lettering 'EAST INDIES SUGAR Not Made By SLAVES'
Stoneware, brown glazed, c.1822-34
130(dia) × 80mm
Norwich Castle Museum. 37.934

184 (illus. p. 94)
Pair of figure groups, celebrating the end of slavery
Porcelain, painted in enamel colours, Staffordshire, c.1830-40
178mm
NMGM (Liverpool Museum). 1991.23

This pair depicts before and after emancipation. The before group follows a standard abolitionist motif. The after scene shows a freed slave with discarded irons and whip, standing before Britannia, identifiable by her helmet, shield and cornucopia.

185 (illus. p. 95)
Medal, obverse: 'JUBILEE IN COM-MEMORATION OF THE ABOLITION OF SLAVERY IN THE BRITISH COLONIES IN THE REIGN OF WILLIAM IV AUG 1 1834', reverse: freed man, woman and child, raising

189

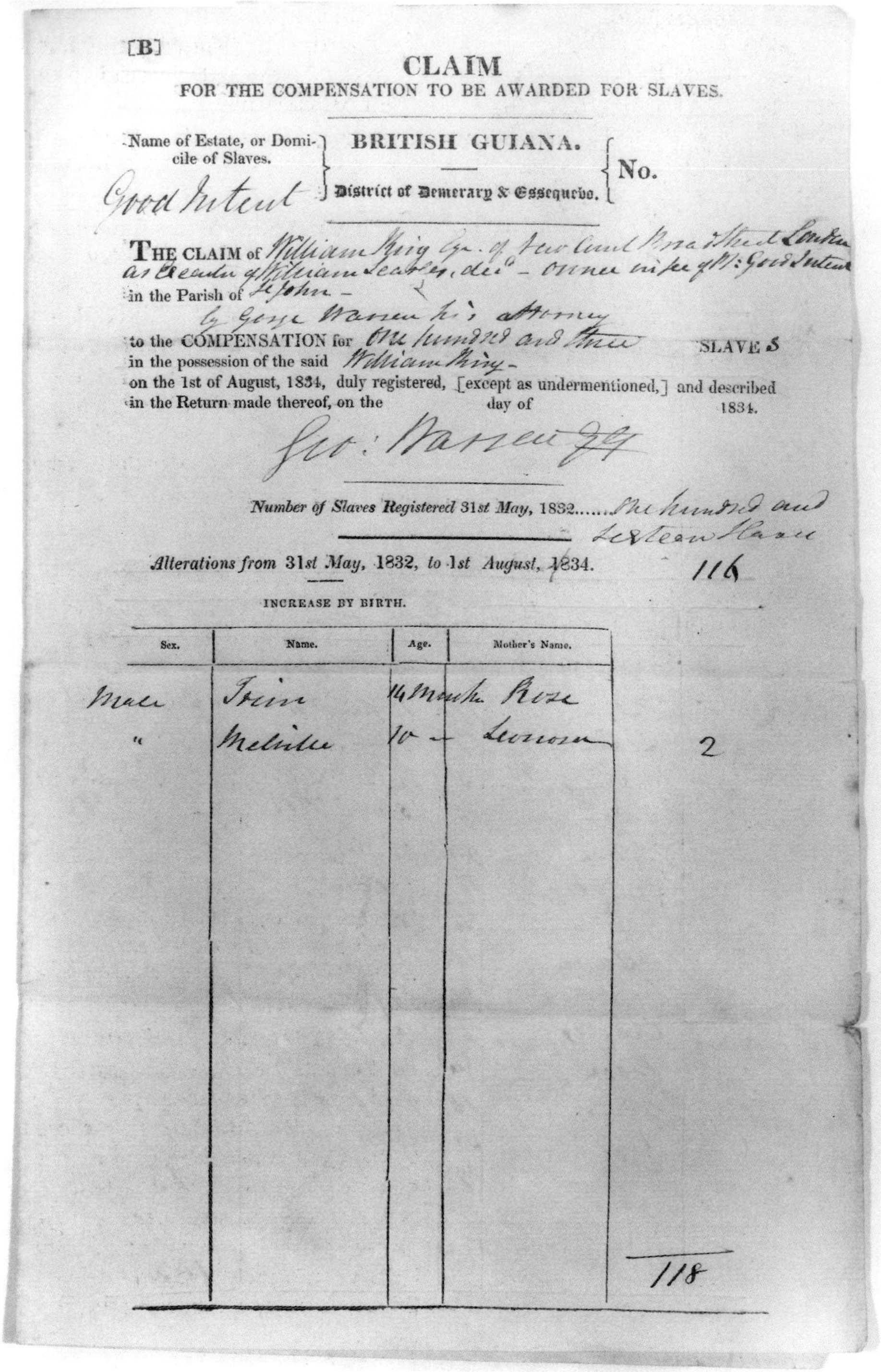

[B]

CLAIM
FOR THE COMPENSATION TO BE AWARDED FOR SLAVES.

Name of Estate, or Domicile of Slaves. — **BRITISH GUIANA.** — No.

District of Demerary & Essequebo.

Good Intent

THE CLAIM of *William King Esq. of New and Broad Street London as executor of William Seabrey decd. owner in fee of Pl: Good Intent* in the Parish of *St John —*

by George Warren his Attorney

to the COMPENSATION for *One hundred and three* SLAVES in the possession of the said *William King —* on the 1st of August, 1834, duly registered, [except as undermentioned,] and described in the Return made thereof, on the   day of   1834.

Geo. Warren JY

Number of Slaves Registered 31st May, 1832...... *One hundred and sixteen Slaves*

Alterations from 31st May, 1832, to 1st August, 1834.   116

INCREASE BY BIRTH.

Sex.	Name.	Age.	Mother's Name.	
Male	Trim	14 Months	Rose	
"	Melville	10 —	Leonora	2
				118

arms to heaven 'GIVE GLORY TO GOD'
T. Halliday, 1834
NMGM (Liverpool Museum). 68.219.107

186 (illus. p. 94)
Medal, obverse: 'IN COMMEMORATION OF THE EXTINCTION OF COLONIAL SLAVERY THROUGHOUT THE BRITISH DOMINIONS IN THE REIGN OF WILLIAM THE IV AUGT 1 1834', reverse: freed man standing in sunlight holding broken chains, 'THIS IS THE LORD'S DOING: IT IS MARVELLOUS IN OUR EYES PSALM 118 V.23 JUBILEE AUGT 1 1834'
J. Davis, 1834
NMGM (Liverpool Museum). 50.28.32

187 (illus. p. 95)
Medal, obverse: William IV seated beneath canopy attended by 4 statesmen (Lords Grey, Rusell, Brougham and Althorp) 'I ADVOCATE THE BILL AS A MEASURE OF HUMANITY', reverse: Seven people hands joined dancing around a palm tree, 'SLAVERY ABOLISHED BY GREAT BRITAIN 1834'
Bronze, probably by T. Halliday, 1834
British Museum. M6222

188 (col. illus. p. 54)
Plate with scene of former slave family in front of cabin, 'FREEDOM FIRST OF AUGUST 1838'
White earthenware with blue transfer-printing
265(dia)mm
NMGM (Merseyside Maritime Museum). 1992.128

Although slavery was abolished in the British colonies in 1834, former slaves were indentured as apprentices for a further four years before they were actually free. 1 August 1838 was regarded and celebrated as the first day of freedom.

189
Claim for compensation for loss of 103 slaves, plantation of Good Intent
1 August 1834
335 × 207mm
Hull Museums. Box 10/3

Plantation owners in British colonies were compensated for the so called loss of their slaves when the Emancipation Act was passed.

190
Promissory Note for compensation for emancipated slaves
6 April 1876
330 × 292mm
Museo Universidad de Puerto Rico

191
Electoral tally, obverse:'MILLIONS FOR FREEDOM. NOT ONE PER CENT FOR SLAVERY', reverse: an eagle, 'SUCCESS TO REPUBLICAN PRINCIPLES'
United States of America
NMGM (Liverpool Museum). 15.2.89.424

192 (illus. p. 68)
Token, obverse:'AM I NOT A WOMAN AND A SISTER 1838', reverse: a kneeling woman, 'UNITED STATES OF AMERICA LIBERTY 1838'
United States of America, 1838
NMGM (Liverpool Museum). 15.2.89.304

191

193 (illus. p. 79)
Manuscript chart showing the tracks of a Royal Navy patrol vessel off the West African Coast
Facsimile of chart by Edward Smith, 1843
National Maritime Museum, London. G241 6/9

This chart, which covers the area from Cape St. Bras to Little Fish Bay, probably shows the track of the Royal Navy patrol vessel BITTERN. This 16-gun brig rigged sloop was one of many British Naval ships on the so called African Station charged to capture illegal slavers during the 1840s. The chart includes dates when slave ships were captured.

194 (illus. p. 80)
'THE CELEBRATED PIRATICAL SLAVER L'ANTONIO with other of the black craft lying in the Bonny River'
Engraved by T. G. Dutton after N. M. Condy, 1845
455 × 535mm
NMGM (Merseyside Maritime Museum). 1992.143

195 (illus. p. 123)
BANSHEE
Builders' model, 1863
Scale 1:64, 460 × 1040 × 100mm
NMGM (Merseyside Maritime Museum). 16.9.27.1

The paddle steamer BANSHEE was built in 1863 by Jones, Quiggin & Co. of Liverpool. She was the first of the so called 'Blockade Runners' ordered by the Confererate States to beat the blockade imposed by the Federal Navy during the American Civil War. A number of ships were built for the Confederacy on Merseyside, where there was much support for their cause.

A Select Bibliography

There is a huge literature on the subject of transatlantic slavery and the following is intended as a guide to further reading.

General

Patterson, O., *Slavery and Social Death: A comparative study*, Cambridge MA, 1982

Reynolds, E., *Stand the Storm: A history of the Atlantic slave trade*, 1985

Walvin, J., *Black Ivory: A History of British Slavery*, London 1992

Williams, E., *Capitalism and Slavery*, North Carolina 1944

Documentary Sources

Donnen, E., *Documents Illustrative of the History of the Slave Trade to America*, 4 vols, Washington 1930-35

Edwards, P., *The Life of Olaudah Equiano*, London 1988

Hall, D., *In Miserable Slavery: Thomas Thistlewood in Jamaica, 1750-1786*, London 1989

Martin, B. & Spurrell, M., *The Journal of A Slave Trader, John Newton, 1750-1754*, London 1962

Special Subjects

Anstey, R. & Hair, P.E., *Liverpool, The African Slave Trade and Abolition*, Liverpool 1976

Beckles, H. & Shepherd, V., eds., *Caribbean Slave Society and Economy: A Student Reader*, Kingston and London 1991

Beckles, H., *Natural Rebels: A Social History of Enslaved Black Women in Barbados*, London and New Jersey 1989

Bethell, L., *The Abolition of the Brazilian Slave Trade*, Cambridge 1970

Bush, B., *Slave Women in Caribbean Society, 1650-1858*, London 1990

Cameron, G. and Crook, S., *Liverpool – Capital of the Slave Trade*, Liverpool 1992

Curten, P.D., *The Atlantic Slave Trade: A Census*, Madison 1969

'Dickey Sam', *Liverpool and Slavery. An Historical Account of the Liverpool-African Slave Trade*, Liverpool 1884, reprinted Liverpool 1986

Elder, M., *The Slave Trade and the Economic Development of Lancaster*, Halifax 1992

Fryer, P., *Staying Power: The History of Black People in Britain*, London 1984

Genovese, E.D., *Roll, Jordan, Roll: The World the Slaves Made*, New York 1972

Gillon, W., *A Short History of African Art*, London 1991

Lloyd, C., *The Navy and the Slave Trade: The Suppression of the African Slave Trade in the Nineteenth Century*, London 1949

Lovejoy, P.E., *Transformations in slavery: A history of slavery in Africa*, Cambridge 1983

Manning, P., *Slavery and African Life*, Cambridge 1990

Morgan, K., 'Bristol and the Atlantic trade in the 18th century' in *English Historical Review*, CVII, 1992, pp.626-50

Patterson, O., *The Sociology of Slavery: An Analysis of the Origins, Development and Structure of Negro Slave Society in Jamaica*, London 1967

Postma, J.M., *The Dutch in the Atlantic Slave Trade 1600-1815*, Cambridge 1990

Richardson, D., and Schofield, M.M., 'Whitehaven and the eighteenth-century British Slave Trade' in *Transactions of the Cumberland and Westmoreland Antiquarian and Archaeological Society*, XCII, 1992, pp.183-204

Robertson, C. and Klein, M., eds., *Women and Slavery In Africa*, Wisconsin 1983

Stein, R., *The French Slave Trade in the Eighteenth Century: An Old Regime Business*, Madison 1979

Walvin, J., *Black and White: The Negro and English Society, 1555-1945*, London 1973

Williams, G., *History of the Liverpool Privateers and Letters of Marque with an account of the Liverpool Slave Trade*, London and Liverpool 1897

Photographic Credits

The Editor is grateful to David Flower, Senior Photographer, for photographing most of the NMGM objects for this catalogue and for copying and preparing all the other photography and to Joanne Howdle, Assistant Curator in the Maritime History department, for handling all the administrative work with such patience and efficiency. Credits refer to catalogue numbers.

Index
relating to essays pp 17–126